The Quaker Way

A Rediscovery

T0096981

The
Quaker Way

A Rediscovery

Rex Ambler

CHRISTIAN
ALTERNATIVE

Winchester, UK
Washington, USA

First published by Christian Alternative Books, 2013
Christian Alternative Books is an imprint of John Hunt Publishing Ltd.,
Laurel House, Station Approach,
Alresford, Hants, SO24 9JH, UK
office1@jhpbooks.net
www.johnhuntpublishing.com
www.christian-alternative.com

For distributor details and how to order please visit the 'Ordering' section on our website.

Text copyright: Rex Ambler 2012

ISBN: 978 1 78099 657 8

A CIP catalogue record for this book is available from the British Library.

Design: Stuart Davies

Printed and bound by CPI Group (UK) Ltd, Croydon, CR0 4YY

We operate a distinctive and ethical publishing philosophy in all areas of our business, from our global network of authors to production and worldwide distribution.

CONTENTS

Other books by Rex Ambler

Truth of the Heart: an anthology of George Fox
Light to Live by: an exploration in Quaker spirituality
The End of Words: issues in contemporary Quaker theology
Global Theology: the meaning of faith in the present world crisis
Agenda for Prophets: towards a political theology for Britain
(edited with David Haslam)

Preface

This book started out as a series of talks, intended to communicate as directly as I could what it means to be Quaker and to follow the Quaker way, especially to people who are not Quaker. Some traces of that informality may still be evident. Also, the series was designed to give a picture of Quakerism as a whole, with a logical sequence from one talk to the next, but when I gave a talk I could not be sure that everyone there had heard the previous one. So every talk had to make sense by itself. This is still partly true. It is possible to read any chapter without having read the ones before. This might be helpful if there are one or two subjects you particularly want to study, but it means that others of you who read the whole thing will have to be patient as I repeat some basic themes of the book.

The talks were given on a number of occasions, in different places, usually at lunchtime during the course of a week. They were public talks, widely advertised, and they were followed by lively discussion over soup and bread. They took some organizing. So I want to thank those people who made them possible: Keith Triplett first of all, for coming up with the idea of the talks, Mo Kelly who arranged for them to take place in Lancaster, England, Anthony Buxton similarly in Edinburgh, Scotland, and Fran Woolgrove in my local town of Kendal. I want to thank those friends too who read through the text as I rewrote it for the book and suggested improvements: Elizabeth Jones, Mel Keiser, and my wife Catherine King Ambler. Jane Holmes, with her unusual computer skills and generosity with time, made the text presentable for the printers.

Abbreviations

EQW
Early Quaker Writings: 1650-1700, ed. Hugh Barbour and Arthur O. Roberts, Eerdmans Pub Co, Grand Rapids, Michigan, 1973 (2nd edition, Pendle Hill Pub, Pennsylvania, 2004).

QFP
Quaker Faith and Practice: the book of Christian discipline of the Yearly Meeting of the Religious Society of Friends (Quakers) in Britain, 4th edition, 1995/2008.

REB
The Revised English Bible, Oxford University Press, 1992.

TOTH
Truth of the Heart: an anthology of George Fox 1624-1691, edited and annotated by Rex Ambler, with a translation into modern English, Quaker Books, 2nd edition 2007.

Introduction

I would like in this book to explain the Quaker way, as far as that is possible. It will not be easy. The Quaker way, after all, is based on a practice of silence, the deliberate letting go of words and ideas. It is an attempt to get beyond all the things we say and write about our life to a direct experience of it. Yet, as we shall see, there is some point in trying to explain why we do this. If we cannot provide a rational case for the Quaker way, we can at least point to those human experiences that help to make sense of it and persuade of its rightness. And we Quakers are confident that everyone has some awareness, some inkling, of the experience we take most seriously, the experience that takes us beyond all words to an encounter with life in the silence. But how to evoke that awareness? Part of the answer is to encourage people to try the practice for themselves, to attend a Quaker meeting for example, and see what the experience yields. But another part of the answer is to attempt to describe the experience, and to try to explain why it is important, how it can be gained, and what difference it makes to our lives and to our engagement with the world. I can only hope that, in offering such an account, I will find echoes in your own experience, that my 'testimony', as we Quakers like to say, 'will answer that of God in everyone.'

I will not assume that you know about the Quaker way already, only that you are interested, and interested enough to want to go deep, to get as far as possible to the core of the matter. In that respect I hope that what I say will be of interest to you even if you are a Quaker. I hope indeed that it will help you or challenge you to think deeply or differently about the Quaker way and to become more conscious of what it is we're committed to and why.

These two aims may seem to be at odds, but my sense is that many people today are interested in Quakerism because of the profound possibilities it offers to people who are looking for something different, perhaps something more real or relevant. They might be a lot more interested if they could understand what those possibilities are. There are also many Quakers who have still not found that depth themselves, though they came to Quakers looking for just that. (This was for many years true of me, and it is because it was a struggle for me to find the depth I was looking for that I feel motivated to communicate my understanding to others.) And others, who have found what they were looking for, may be lost for words when asked to explain what that is. So I am confident that a probing inquiry into what the Quaker way is might be of interest to many different kinds of people.

Making sense of the Quaker way

My probing for this book began five years ago when I was asked by my own Quaker Meeting to give a series of talks on 'The Quaker Way of Doing Things.' Their concern was that many people had started to attend the meeting who were very puzzled by the way we did things. We sat in silence for a whole hour, for example, and no one led the meeting or explained what was happening (or not happening!). There were also members who were still puzzled after many years about why we adopted such a slow and cumbersome process in coming to decisions together. They could only see the traditional language about 'being led' and 'waiting in the light' as at best vacuous phrases for thinking about a difficult matter, or at worst a refusal to think seriously at all. So I was challenged to offer some rationale for these and other strange practices of Friends. In thinking about them, however, I came to realize that an historical or descriptive explanation would not really answer the questions being put. If I explained what was set down in the official Book of Discipline, *Quaker Faith and Practice*, I could still be asked why it was set down, and indeed, whether it was a fundamentally good thing that it had been set down. The question Why? kept coming back at me. Why, for example, do we sit in silence? Why do we not vote in Meetings for Business? Why do we insist on a nonviolent resolution to all conflicts? What was being asked in my Meeting and what I found I was asking myself required a deeper search into Quaker ways and practices. In fact, it required a search into The Quaker Way itself. That changes the meaning of the word, of course. 'The way' is no longer a way of doing things, a particular procedure that we follow because it seems to work for us. It is more a way *to* something. A way to life, or liberty or happiness, maybe. There are many different ways to life and liberty, as we are all well aware, and the Quaker way is merely one. But it is distinctive, if not entirely unique. It has its own rationale, its own distinctive insight and sense of direction. It is aiming for something that is of fundamental concern to every human being, yet its chosen way of getting there is particular. It may not appeal to everybody, compared with other ways on offer, but it might appeal to many more than follow it now if it were better known and understood. So I see the challenge to me in writing this book is to describe that Quaker way of life and at the same time to make sense of it.

But the more mundane questions still remain. Questions about how we make decisions or how we try to change things don't fall into the background. The reason for this, as I have come to understand it, is that the Quaker way of life, the Quaker way *to* life, is essentially practical. Whatever else we do as Quakers – talking, reading, gardening, playing music, whatever – we come back to the practice again and again.[1] That attitude itself needs some explaining, and it is one of the first things I will try to do. But notice here the difficulty it creates.

The Quaker way of life is very simple, once you grasp it, but actually grasping it may not be so easy. It is so *different* from other ways of doings things, though superficially it may seem familiar. It may seem like an idealistic way of life, even possibly a highly moral one, engaged with great issues of peace and social justice. But when we look closely we notice that Quaker meetings are remarkably passive, and that when Quakers do engage with the world they take an awful long time to find out what to do. Everyone, for example, has to be kept on board and no-one must be left disgruntled or side-lined. The actions themselves, when Quakers finally get round to them, are so gentle, so benign, that we may wonder how they could ever make a difference. Are Quakers naïve, failing to understand the world they live in, or are they so radical they leave the rest of us standing?

Another difficulty is that, unlike most other religious groups we may know of, their way is *not based on an official teaching*, a doctrine. There is no creed, or statement of belief. Quakers haven't first of all worked out what they believe, or ought to believe, and then attempted to put it into practice. They start at the other end. They practice it first, then they work out how best to understand it or communicate it. Even then, they don't formulate their understanding as 'beliefs'. Why should they? If they've learnt from the practice, they know it in their hearts. And if it works in practice, why bother with formulation in words? I'll try to explain that later, but you can see already how such an idea could backfire. They could become so occupied with the doing that they don't bother even with the understanding. They may then soon find that they don't really understand what they are doing, and why! This is something of a problem for Quakers today. Many of them will find it difficult to explain why they do what they do: they just 'get on with it' and not worry too much about why and how, until, of course, they meet some confusion or difference of opinion on what they should do next.

So I see my task in this book as trying to make sense of what Quakers do by confronting three difficulties:

1. The Quaker way is *different*, and radical.
2. It is not based on ideas or *beliefs*, so it is not easily

expressed this way either.

3. It has not been well *understood*, even by Quakers themselves, since they're focused on the doing.

So Quakers have some explaining to do. I have spent my professional life, as a theologian, trying to explain and interpret religious ideas and practices, so it was natural for me to want to get to work theologically on these Quaker conundrums. But I hesitated. The categories that I normally applied in interpreting religion didn't seem to fit. There was an elusive quality to the Quaker life which could not be got at with the words I was used to employing, and it was this very thing, I realized, that really appealed to me and drew me in. I didn't want to spoil it. It took me some ten years to feel confident that I could talk about the Quaker faith in an intellectually coherent way.[2] But I wasn't entirely satisfied even then. I felt that the practice of 'silent waiting', which is central for Quakers, was all too fuzzy in my description. And, to be honest, it was all too fuzzy in my own experience. It was only when I came to study the early Quaker writings that I discovered what the practice was meant to be, that is, what was meant to happen in the 'silent waiting' and how this could relate to our experience of everyday life. I wrote about this too, and about my own experience of trying out the practice as the early Friends described it.[3] But that was specifically about the core practice, the meditation in silence. It became clear to me though, as I hint in that book, that this deepening of the practice has implications for our understanding of Quaker life as a whole. This has been confirmed as I have shared the practice with others. In a conscious revival of the old practice, in what has now become known as Experiment with Light, Quakers have discovered a greater understanding both of themselves, which is their first concern, and of the Quaker way on which they are set.[4] So I'm drawing on this contemporary experience, as well as on early Friends' writings, in offering this explanation of what

Quakers do.

The explanation may not reflect exactly what many Quakers today say and think. It is not, in that sense, an account of what most Quakers today consciously do as Quakers. It is more probing, more searching, and therefore, I hope, more challenging. It is asking about the underlying meaning of our practice, which may have been forgotten even while the practice itself continues. It is, among other things therefore, an invitation to recover the original vision, but in a way that answers the needs and possibilities of our own generation.

So let us let us begin our enquiry with an account of what Quakers generally do.

The practice

The core practice of Friends in meeting together has not funda-mentally changed in 350 years. They sit in silence together for an hour or so, standing up to speak only if they are led to do so, and then only to share some insight which they sense will be of value to others. If they gain insight from this time together, as they hope to, they try to put it into practice in their everyday life. They try to be 'faithful' to what they have learned. If their insight involves other people, they may share it with them and see if they can do something together. If a decision has to be made by the whole group of Friends, the Meeting, they will wait in silence together, again, to discern what has to be done. And all the while they are bearing in mind how this impacts on the world around them. What can they do or say that will help others in their need or confusion? One thing they do know. The best they can do for others is to live according to the 'light' they have in them. Their lives will then bear 'testimony' to what others need to know. In particular, they will do no harm to others, but seek always positively to help them, otherwise they will undermine the process that makes for peace and wholeness. How precisely they are to help in any given situation has to be worked out, to be 'discerned', in that situation. They trust that they will be 'led', and that in following their leading they will do some good. That is their faith.

I hope this will stand as a brief and fair account of the Quaker way, as it has been followed since the seventeeth century. There have of course been many variations on it during that time, from rule-bound conformity to evangelical fervour, but there is also a remarkable continuity[5]. And there is a basic coherence and simplicity to it. People live as they are led. It is expressed also in the first Advice in our Book of Discipline, now published as *Quaker Faith and Practice*,[6] which echoes advice that has been given by the Society of Friends for most of its history:

> Take heed, dear Friends, to the promptings of love and truth in your hearts. Trust them as the leadings of God, whose Light shows us our darkness and leads us to new life.

I will come back to that Advice again, because it expresses so well the guidance we give ourselves, and others, on how we are to find the good life. But I can see that it might strike some people, when they read it for the first time, as very bad advice. It seems to be suggesting that we follow our hearts instead of our heads, and, even worse, that we treat our own inner promptings as the voice of God.

That criticism was expressed by the official rulebook of the Church of England, once it had been restored in 1662 after the revolutionary surges of the previous twenty years. *The Book of Common Prayer* refers to the Quakers, obliquely, in the Preface. It is pleased to announce that the old:

> Forms of Divine worship... do yet stand firm and unshaken, notwithstanding all the vain attempts and impetuous assaults made against it, by such men as are given to change, and have always discovered a greater regard to their own private

fancies and interests, than to that duty they owe to the publick.[7]

The implication is that these reckless people are not only self-centred but also irresponsible, indifferent to the public good. And being driven by 'fancies' they would be indifferent to the rules and procedures that had been laid down by authority. They were a threat to the establishment. This attitude to Friends prevailed and they were therefore, at the instigation of leaders of the church, persecuted severely by the State for some twenty five years. That persecution was hardly just or right, but the worries that led to it were not inappropriate. Friends had a case to answer.

And Friends have a case to answer today. Not that they are seen as a threat now. But they are seen by many people to be unreliable in another way: they rely on inner impulses which they take, supposedly, to be an infallible guide to living. They are living against the grain of society, which seeks to promote the common good by appeal to the facts, good argument and a sense of what human beings really want. Modern society is upfront, rational and devoted to common sense. Friends, by contrast, seem to be relying on impulses that moderns can only regard with suspicion. Friends even identify these impulses, apparently, with the voice of God. People who hear voices in their head and take them as final are not normally taken seriously; they may even be thought to be dangerous, if only to themselves. Are Quakers then flirting with something quite dodgy? They may be admired by some for their idealism, but their methods and procedures seem questionable, to say the least.

These arguments need to be taken seriously, but they show how easy it is to misunderstand the Quaker way and align it with something else. My concern here is, not so much to silence criticism, which on the whole must be healthy, but to deepen understanding. We need to ask more precisely: what is really going on when Quakers sit in silence? What are they listening for or waiting for? And why do they take these inner 'promptings' so seriously?

Let me give a brief answer to these questions first of all. It will need to be backed up and explained later, but a brief summary now should give our discussion a sense of direction. And it should help us to define the further questions that we will need to ask to get a clearer understanding.

Quakers sit in silence because they want to know something that words cannot tell them. They want to feel something or become aware of something so that they can really make a connection with it. It is something fundamental to their life, they know that, indeed it is the underlying reality of their life, but they are not normally aware of it. They are preoccupied with other things. They are taken up, like others, with the relatively shallow things of life, encouraged by the media and contemporary culture generally, and they hardly feel the depth of it all. So they feel the loss, the distance, and want somehow to get close to this deeper reality. They want to become 'the Friends of Truth', as they liked to call themselves at the beginning. Not any truth, but a truth that relates specifically to their deepest felt needs, and to the needs of the world. They are looking for a truth by which to live,[8] that is, a sense of reality that tells them who they are and how they should live. They want the truth in this sense because that is the only basis on which they could expect to enjoy life to the full and to contribute to life. Part of the reality of their life, of course, is their relationship with one another and with other people, both near and far. So they want to 'discern' what happens between people, what makes for a good life together, and what makes for a bad one. They want to learn in their own experience how relationships that are broken can be mended, how conflicts can be resolved, and how 'the Friends of Truth' can work together to make these things happen in the world.

This is the brief answer. This is the aspiration, at least, that leads them to do the unusual things they do. Like many other people, they experience life as disconnected, broken, at odds.

They feel basically dissatisfied with life as it is generally lived, unhappy with the way people treat one another, and unhappy with themselves. But they know intuitively that it doesn't have to be like this, that there is an underlying unity and meaning in life, if only they could find it. They don't want to give in to the pessimism that says this is all it ever can be, yet on the other hand they can't accept the optimism that pretends that life is other than it is. They want the truth about life. Risky as it may be, they want to find out how things really are, because they sense, they hope, that the truth will give meaning to their lives and make them whole.

But what is meant by truth here? It doesn't seem to mean what we normally mean by it. No, indeed. So it is a good point on which to begin our exploration. Other questions we have about this Way will become a lot clearer, and easier to resolve, if we can first be clear about this Quaker understanding of truth.

Chapter one

Finding the truth

What is truth?

We are very conditioned these days by the scientific idea of truth. We think that truth is simply the facts, and that you can only claim to have the truth when you can prove what you say, point to the evidence that is there for everybody to see. This is what is called objective truth, and it is very fundamental to our modern way of life; it has in fact enabled us to make great progress socially and technologically. But it is not the only truth we need. We also need a truth about ourselves, our own particular experience of life and our relationships with other people. There is much puzzlement about these basic experiences of life, much confusion and uncertainty. We find it difficult to understand why we are so often unhappy or dissatisfied with life, why people generally suffer so much, or make others suffer, and what sense we can make of our life when it will inevitably be taken away from us. Perhaps the deepest puzzlement is about who we ourselves really are. Do we really know ourselves as we are? Is there perhaps a real self, behind this mask I wear in my everyday life, or am I simply what I and others have decided I am?

Now these are questions of truth, but the truth in question is not the kind you could discover from a scientific investigation. Sciences deal with objects out there, quite separate from me as the observer or researcher. These personal questions are inescapably about me. To answer them, if an answer is to be found, I must become more fully aware of myself, and of the people I share my life with. This kind of truth is more direct and intimate, more all-embracing than the truth that gives you facts. Let's call it *personal truth*, to distinguish it from scientific and factual truth.

This is the kind of truth we can get from reading novels or watching films, when we are deeply moved by what we see happening and recognize something of our own experience in it. We don't normally speak of this as truth, but if as a result of this experience we have got to know our own life better it surely has to be called truth. The same could be said of art and music, which dispense with words altogether. Quite apart from the enjoyment we may get from seeing the pictures or listening to the sounds, we may find our own experience of life being mirrored back to us. So we can find them affirming of life, or challenging, and we know in our hearts that that is the reason we want to see and hear these things.

Is it possible, though, to become aware of ourselves directly, without the intervention of music, art, films and such like? Can we find out who we are, and what is really going on for us, by looking and seeing for ourselves? Is personal truth accessible in this way? These are questions the first Quakers asked, in the seventeenth century, and we could say their movement began when they began to find answers to these questions.

The Quaker quest

George Fox, the recognized leader of the movement, spent many years as a young man travelling from place to place, from preacher to preacher, trying to find the truth behind the many competing ideas of his time. But none, he said, 'spoke to his condition'. He discovered in later years why this was. The preachers were relying on a book to give them knowledge, the Bible, but they had to interpret the book themselves and to apply it to the experience of their hearers. What they said in these long sermons, and wrote in their even longer books, was often impressive. They were making a very serious attempt to understand human life and its dilemmas on the basis of a revelation of God in the past. But that was the problem. What had been said in the past, even if it had come from a profound experience of God, did not necessarily reflect the experience of people living much later. And if the preacher did not have a comparable experience himself he was in no position to interpret that ancient text for the people of his own time. Some of these Puritan preachers were aware of this problem and they tried to overcome it by urging their hearers to pray for the experience that would make sense of it all. Most of them however tried to make sense of it themselves and urged their hearers simply to 'believe the word of God' as it had been expounded to them. But inevitably, as you can appreciate, it gave rise to doubt and uncertainty. How do we know this is God's word to us? people asked. And how can we make sense of it if we have no experience of hearing God speak to us? Simply believing what had been said didn't seem to help, because it set up a conflict between what people held to be true in their minds and what they experienced of life in their hearts. For the same reason, they found it impossible to live out the life they professed to believe in, as did the preachers and professors who had set out these ideas so impressively. To many people – including those who were later to become Quakers – there seemed to be an unbridgeable gulf between the words that told them the truth about life and their own actual experience of life. What, then, was the point of believing? In fact it seemed to make matters worse. It persuaded them to think that they had the truth, when they only had a description of it. They had a picture, we might say, and they mistook the picture for reality. The picture therefore got in the way. It prevented them from seeing reality with their own eyes. It alienated them from the very thing they most wanted and needed to know.

It was this uncomfortable sense of unreality and alienation that alerted the first Friends to look for something different. The tragedy of the situation was well described by one of the most articulate of the first Friends, Isaac Penington, in 1675. He was referring to people who accepted orthodox beliefs about Christ (almost everybody in the country did at that time) but didn't know the reality of Christ in themselves:

> The historical relation concerning Christ is generally believed and received by all sorts that pretend to Christianity. His death, his miracles, his rising, his ascending, his interceding, etc. is generally believed by all people; but the mystery they miss of, the hidden life they are not acquainted with, but alienated from the life of God, in the midst of their literal owning and acknowledging of these things.... The knowledge of these, without the knowledge of the mystery, is not sufficient to bring them unto God; for many set up that which they gather and comprehend from the relation concerning these things [i.e. being told about them], instead of the thing itself, and so never come to a sense of their need of the thing itself, nay, not so far as rightly to seek after it.[9]

An experiment in silence

The challenge for those early Quakers, who understood all this, was how to find a viable alternative. How were they to discover this reality that promised to make sense of their lives and which had been so badly obscured by all the worthy attempts to define it in words? And if they did find this more elusive reality, would it in fact help them? Would it make sense of their life, and would it respond to their deeply felt needs and desires? All this was uncertain. Moreover there was a fear that in opposing human words they would be opposing the Word of God. The teaching of that time, after all, was almost entirely based on the Bible, which was regarded as the one sure source of the truth that people most deeply sought. The preachers and teachers were merely interpreters of 'God's Word'. But that claim, after the ravages of Civil War and the failures of the Commonwealth, was already beginning to wear thin. The preachers and politicians had obviously not found a truth that could serve the national interest, either politically or religiously. They couldn't even agree among themselves as to what the Bible meant. So there was reason to be sceptical. There was also reason to be hopeful that an alternative could be found, and that it wouldn't fly in the face of the God they wished to know. What might that be?

Those who were disillusioned with the teaching of their time could at least recognize that they must have had *some* rudimentary knowledge of what they were looking for, otherwise they wouldn't have realised that the official teaching had missed it, or muffled it. Something in their experience enabled them to see what was right and appropriate. Perhaps if they gave more attention to their experience, they could make some real progress.

Something similar was happening in other spheres of life, as people came to realize that the long-standing authorities which ruled their lives could possibly get it all wrong. This had happened with the king, Charles I, when he so blatantly defied his people's interest and even declared war on them. His claim to rule 'by divine right' was publicly shown to be wrong, and the people, realizing this, decided to take government into their own hands. This was the beginning of what we now understand as democracy. In science, the teaching of the philosophers, based always on the most ancient texts, had been found to contradict what ordinary people could now observe for themselves. Anybody could now buy a telescope and do what Galileo had done, look at the stars and see for themselves how they actually moved. In almost every area of life people were beginning to distrust authority, what had been handed down in books to be accepted without question, and they were beginning to rely on experience, that is, on the reality that persuaded them that authority had failed to get it right.

In religion, however, the stakes were much higher. Seekers after truth would have to be brave. What was to be tested in experience was the reality of human life itself. People would have to experiment, not with the physical world around them, or with the political structures they used to govern their lives, but directly with themselves. It wasn't a foregone conclusion, either, that in investigating their own lives they would find a reality they could finally trust, or even a reality that was benign and sensitive to their need. A contemporary of the first Quakers, Thomas Hobbes, published a book in 1651 in which he described human life as so dark and dangerous that it needed political force to contain it:

> During the time men live without a common power to keep them all in awe, they are in that condition which is called war; and such a war as is of every man against every man... the nature of war consisteth not in actual fighting, but in the known disposition thereto during all the time there is no assurance to the contrary.[10]

In such a situation the life of human beings is 'solitary, poor, nasty, brutish and short'.[11]

But the Quaker experiment came up with a very different finding. George Fox gives us the earliest example of their discovery, referring to an event in 1647 when he was still in his early twenties:

> As I had forsaken the priests, so I left the separate preachers also, and those called the most experienced people; for I saw there was none among them all that could speak to my condition. And when all my hopes in them and in all men were gone, so that I had nothing outwardly to help me, nor could tell me what to do; then, O then I heard a voice which said, 'There is one, even Christ Jesus, that can speak to thy condition'. When I heard it, my heart did leap for joy... Jesus Christ... enlightens, and gives grace, faith and power. Thus when God doth work, who shall let it [who can stop it]? This I knew experimentally.[12]

This was a voice within him. Nothing external, 'outward', had been able to 'speak to his condition'. No words had been able to match his experience as he knew it for himself, though clearly he knew enough of his experience to know that the words didn't fit. Why had he not trusted this inner knowledge before? Because, he seems to say, he had been stuck on the words of the priests and preachers.[13] He had been expecting truth to be conveyed to him by them. It was only when he 'had forsaken the priests' that he heard another kind of voice, within him. He had been disappointed by the preachers for years, as he tells us in the Journal, but he still held on to the belief that one or other of them would eventually come up with the truth. The truth, he believed, must come in the form of words. But the disappointment eventually became too much, too comprehensive, and he finally 'gave up'. This must have been a point of despair. He had wanted desperately to find the reality he could trust to give him a sense of who he was and what he was to do. Every attempt had failed. But at that point, feeling utterly alone and deserted, he sensed something in him which began to tell him what he needed to hear. (Was this the same inner sense that had told him before that the religious teaching he had heard did not match his experience? Was that implicit sense now becoming explicit?) He was being told to listen to something deeper within him that could communicate the whole truth that he desired to know, but it would do this, not by giving him just another set of words, but by enabling him *to see*. It 'enlightens', he says confidently. It was making him aware of the reality of his life, which had previously been covered by the verbal description. But what precisely was enabling him to 'see'? It was obviously not his normal self that was talking, not his own reason or imagination. It was like another self, another spirit than the one he was familiar with. He could only think that this inner self or spirit was Jesus Christ himself, the one whom the Bible describes as the very word and spirit of God.

And *what* precisely was he enabled to see? He describes an experience later that year, which is not very promising:

> But oh, then did I see my troubles, trials and temptations more than I had ever done! As the light appeared, all appeared that is out of the light, darkness, death, temptation, the unrighteous, the ungodly; all was manifest and seen in the light. And then the spiritual discerning came into me, by which I did discern my own thoughts, groans and sighs, and what it was that did veil me, and what it was that did open me.[14]

This sounds more like the image of human life projected by Thomas Hobbes', 'nasty, brutish and short'. But look at it more closely. It is not all darkness and death. There is also 'the light' which enables him to see the darkness and death. So there is something in him which is uncontaminated by the blight on human affairs and which is free from the pressures of self-interest and pretence. It is concerned with truth. The second thing to note is that as well as exposing the reality of his life, in all its unsavoury detail, it shows how he got into this mess and how he can get out of it – 'what it was that did veil me, and what it was that did open me.' This is what gives him some leverage in the situation. He can now understand what he has done with his life, so that he is free to live it differently. He is not trapped in a depraved human nature, as he had been taught to believe, bound to live a futile and guilt-ridden life for the rest of his days. He had within him, deep down, the resources to live as he really wanted to live. Or rather, one deep, divine resource which would give him all the insight, 'faith, grace and power' that he needed. The third thing to note is that what the light revealed to him first of all was something on which he could immediately take action – himself. It would show him many other things later as and when he was able to receive these new insights – the Journal tells us much about these 'openings' – but none of this would be possible until he had seen the truth about himself and done something about it. He would have to recognize the wrong and foolish things he had done, and why, so that he could find a new way to live and a new 'grace and power' to live it. Then he would be free to see what was really going on in the world around him.

So what Fox discovered in this daring experiment is that you *can* make contact with the deep reality of your life, and that it *is* responsive to your need and the need of the world. As we would say, the experiment worked.

This discovery or disclosure seems to have happened quite unexpectedly to George Fox. But he soon found that he was able to guide people into a similar experience. As he returned to that inner silence again and again, he was able to discern *how* the voice spoke to him and how the light enlightened him. He observed time and again what happened to him when he did this or did that, and on that basis he was able to recommend to others what they should do. When he was still and silent, for example, he was more able to hear something deep within him, because his own thoughts and fancies would have quietened down. If he closed his eyes and waited for the truth he was concerned with to reveal itself to him, he would 'see' what he needed to see: a 'light' within him would show it up.

That then became the basis of his message. He would urge people to give up their reliance on books and the people who tried to interpret them, and to turn instead to a source of insight and understanding inside them. But that also meant giving up thought and imagination, at least for this special time of meditation, for these too were governed by words and images, and would inevitably distract them from the direct experience they needed. He made this clear in an early tract of 1657, 'To all the People on the Earth', but addressed particularly to those who valued reason and debate above all on these things:

All you that be in your own wisdom and in your own reason, you tell that silent waiting upon God is famine to you; it is a strange life to you to come to be silent, you must come into a new world. Now you must die in the silence, die from the wisdom, die from the knowledge, die from the reason, and die from the understanding.[15]

That was a tough demand to make on the intellectuals of his day, who lived by their words, but he could see that it was necessary if they were to break through into immediacy and discover truth for themselves. The benefit of this 'strange life' of silence would make the sacrifice worth it, as he says in the same epistle:

Here every spirit comes to have a particular satisfaction and quietness in his own mind, and here the weary come to have rest in Christ... Such shall find mercy of God when their minds are guided up unto God and their spirits and minds are quieted in silent waiting upon God. In one half hour they have more peace and satisfaction than they have had from all other teachers of the world all their lifetime.[16]

We can now see why the practice of silent waiting was so important, and remains so. It makes possible a way of seeing reality that takes us beyond the limits of words. Words are helpful up to a point. They indicate, perhaps, the experience we might undergo for ourselves, or the actions we might take, or the fine example of others' lives. But they don't of themselves enable us to recognise and face and come to terms with the reality of our own life. In fact, they tend to hinder that process. To come to a direct knowledge of truth we have to (temporarily at least) let go of any words that we believed might have described it. We have to be silent and wordless even in our thoughts. Then another kind of awareness will arise, quite different from our normal, wordy ideas. So Fox urges us:

Be still and cool in thy own mind and spirit from thy own thoughts, and then thou wilt feel the principle of God to turn thy mind to the Lord God, whereby thou wilt receive his strength and power from whence life comes... therefore be still a while from thy own thoughts, searching, seeking, desires and imaginations, and be stayed in the principle of God in thee, to stay thy mind upon God, up to God.[17]

Therefore all now awake from sleep and see where you are. Let the light of Jesus Christ, that shine in every one of your consciences, search you thoroughly, and it will let you clearly see.[18]

Here we might see things as they are, free from the constructions we like to put on them. We get to a new kind of objectivity – not the 'facts' of science, which concern objects 'out there' quite independent of 'me', but the reality of our own experience, independent of what others (out there) have taught us, or our own thoughts and feelings might have persuaded us to believe.[19]

But why, we might ask, is it so difficult to recognize and accept our own experience? It sounds like the easiest thing in the world, and also the most fundamental. Indeed it is. And yet there is a huge obstacle in our way.

The pretensions of the ego

There was a hint of this problem in two of the quotations I gave from Fox. He called on Lady Claypool to 'be still and cool in thy own mind and spirit from *thy own* thoughts.' He warned the proud intellectuals to be wary of their 'own wisdom' and their 'own reason', suggesting that that proud self 'had to die.' At another time – one of the last Epistles he wrote - he celebrated the truth that liberates people because it makes them 'universal [in their outlook], to live out of narrowness and self, and deny it.'[20] So the self is a problem. Even when it's thinking and reasoning (using words in the most disciplined way) it can get things badly wrong. How are we to understand this?

Early Friends talked a lot about self-will, the tendency of the self to assert itself. We can understand this better in modern terms by speaking of the pretensions of the ego. The ego is our self as we think of it, our sense of identity. It is not the whole me or the true me, but the me I am conscious of, the me I want to convey to the rest of the world. Can this be a problem?

We need a sense of self, of course, in order to function at all. But we do not know ourselves thoroughly, so any self-image we devise – or take over from others – will be highly selective. It will give us what we need for the practical purpose of getting on with others. But there's the rub. What will others think of us? Will they want to support us and help us? Or will they be antagonistic or indifferent? Our fate seems to depend on what others think. So without a good self-image we feel naked and vulnerable. This underlying anxiety is no doubt what makes the image so important to us, yet our holding on to the image creates more anxiety, because the image never quite fits the reality, as we already know at some level, even if we constantly tell ourselves otherwise. The stories we tell of our life, even to ourselves, are not only selective, but also somewhat exaggerated if not actually deceitful. The way we dress and conduct ourselves too, the way we look at others (or ignore them), talk to them and treat them, communicates to them how we want to be seen (rather than how we actually are). This may seem to us a fairly innocent quirk of human nature, if we are aware of it at all, but Friends have always regarded it as a serious problem. The danger is not that we tell stories about ourselves, or that we entertain an image of ourselves, both of which are necessary and helpful, but that we identify with the image, this flat, two-dimensional picture. We say, and think, this is the real me. But it is not of course. It is a pretension, a fiction, in so far as we identify with it. It has to be maintained always against the grain of reality. And this, Friends have recognized, is one of the sources, perhaps the primary source, of the miseries that we create for ourselves and for others.

The Quaker psychologist Adam Curle describes the situation as follows:

> A great deal of human behaviour is influenced by our need to have a good image of our own selves. We create for ourselves a mask representing what we would like to show to others, and to ourselves. To complement the mask is what I would call the mirage. The popular belief is that mirages are beautiful visions of palm trees and water, but anyone who has travelled in deserts knows that they live up to their dictionary definition of a false image. Mirages are shimmering stretches of livid waste. In my terms, the mirage is what we see when we squint through the slits in the mask. In order to maintain the mask, to have a gratifying self-image, we need a comparably unattractive one of our rivals or enemies. Upon them we project all the flaws and vices we fear in ourselves and try unconsciously to conceal by the mask mechanism. This gives rise to what has been termed the mirror effect, in which each protagonist sees the other in the same unfavourable light in which he himself is seen. In this way most conflicts are unreasonably exacerbated while the mutually distorted perceptions impede adequate communications, which is an essential preliminary to any accord.[21]

The first Quakers were not the first to recognize the self as a problem. Many thinkers of that time were making the same observation. The Puritans, who were the dominant intellectuals in Britain, saw the self as rebellious. The poet Milton described the rebellion dramatically in his *Paradise Lost*: God had told the first man and woman how to live, but they defied him, disobeyed his command and brought misery on themselves and

the rest of the world. Every human in the world was now prede-
termined to rebel. The Puritan answer to this plight was to
repress the cause of the trouble, the stubborn self, though it was
a life-long struggle which never quite succeeded. Their only hope
of salvation was that finally, after death, they would be forgiven
by God and received into his presence. The Quaker answer was
very different, and derived from their discovery of what
happened in silent waiting. The self was indeed stubborn, but its
assertiveness was due to a profound misunderstanding. The self
thinks it is alone and needs to fight its corner. But this is an
illusion created by anxiety. The self, that is the true self, is in fact
connected with others, and indeed with the whole creation and
with its mysterious origin in God. But it cannot see this because
it has identified with an image, an idea. Feeling therefore alone
and vulnerable, it tries to make itself safe and secure, linking up
with others with a similar interest and power to sustain
themselves, accumulating wealth and status, and above all
asserting its own interests as primary. When confronted by
authorities who deny those interests, even if the authority is God,
it will naturally 'rebel'. But that is not the main problem. The
problem is that the self refused to accept its actual situation, the
truth, and opted for a story or image instead. It is living a fiction.

What is needed therefore is that people find the truth again,
accept it, and live their lives on the basis of it. This may seem a
tall order, but we have to remember that 'the truth' as the
Quakers understand it and pursue it is the reality of our own life,
which we are already in some sense aware of, but have denied
and repelled from our consciousness. What we have to do – and
this is the Quaker advice - is stop this activity of telling stories
about ourselves, stop defending ourselves and making up
attractive ideas about ourselves and sit still with the silence – and
with the reality of our life as we gradually become aware of it.
This will be our first and formative experience of 'the truth'.

The difficulty here is not that we cannot find the truth that we need, but that we don't really want it and/or know how to handle it. We had good reasons, no doubt, for repressing much of the reality of our life before, so to let it out into the open again would seem to be dangerous, or at least very unpleasant and unfruitful. This danger is real, of course, and the experience of opening up to the truth can be painful, just because we are so attached to the way we normally think of ourselves. But people who have been through the experience can bear witness that the outcome is well worth the pain. The early Friends emphasised this again and again. They would compare it sometimes to giving birth to a baby, and in a metaphorical sense they were, because they were giving birth to a new self:

> That which calls your minds out of the earth, turns them towards God, where the pure babe is born in the virgin mind.[22]

The light within

Humans cannot of course see the truth about themselves, or about anything else, so long as they are committed to a false image or theory. They will see only what is compatible with the image, the 'mirage', as Adam Curle puts it, that they see through the slits of their 'mask.' If they drop the mask, however, they will see everything differently, including themselves. They will see things as they are, without the distortions created by their egos, both individually and collectively. Moreover, they will see their pretentious egos as *they* are. But is this possible? Can 'egos' see themselves? It sounds like they're chasing their own tails!

That that kind of self-knowledge is possible was, I believe, another important discovery of the first Quakers. They found that when they sat in silence and slowed down the thinking process in their minds, the self began to subside. It was less anxious and assertive. But more than that, an awareness arose within them which seemed to come from outside them, not because it was strange or other-worldly, but because it let them see the whole of their life. They could run their life through like watching a play on the stage. They could focus on any detail that concerned them, or draw back to get a sense of the whole drama. This was a capacity of detachment, an ability to get a distance on the things that normally felt too close for comfort and too close to see. And this detachment enabled them to look at things squarely that they had previously wanted to ignore. They would see the 'darkness, death, and temptations' that Fox talked about, but they wouldn't be fazed by them. They would need courage to face this dark side of their lives, but on the other hand there was less anxiety around it because the anxious self had been allowed to slip into the background. It was possible to say, Yes, this is how things are, this is what I have done, and this is the result. With that being said there is a huge relief and sense of freedom. There is a feeling of *not* being condemned, but rather, surprisingly, of being accepted. They could accept things as they are because they themselves were felt to be ultimately all right. But that sense of being accepted, they found, was dependent on *their* accepting the truth of what they had seen. The one seemed to depend on the other, and *vice versa*.

It was also a new kind of freedom because the self was not now struggling to defend itself or secure itself. It could see what it wanted to see, move as it wanted to move, and so come to a judgement about the situation with real objectivity. Then it was possible to act with confidence, and with good effect.

Also, it was possible in this meditative state to see through the pretensions of the self so that they lose their persuasiveness. They could see the self posturing, fighting its corner, but they could also see the illusion that led them to do this. And an exposure to the truth of its situation was enough for the self, this posturing self, to abandon its pretence. There might be a struggle, of course – our familiar self is not going to give way that easily, but if it is also made aware of the suffering it causes to itself and to others by pursuing this pretence, it may finally give up. And the reward is a discovery of the true self – what I or we have been experiencing all along – and the discovery of our real connection with others and with life.

The discovery may not come all at once, of course. It may take a long time, a lifetime even. But new insight is always possible, once we accept the insights we have already been given. As with George Fox, one 'opening' leads to another. And we can be assured that, whatever situation we are in, we have a capacity deep within us to see the truth of our situation, to wake up to who we are and where we are, and to do what we know in our hearts to be the right thing. To realize that potential within us, to become what we know in some sense we are meant to become, we know that we simply have to act on 'the promptings of love and truth in our hearts', and to see where they lead. The rest will then follow quite naturally.

Chapter two

Looking for God

The point of silence, as we have considered it so far, is to gain awareness. This, we might say, is the beginning of the Quaker way. And the first thing we need to become aware of in the Quaker way is ourselves. We have to break through the ideas and images we have constructed of ourselves to something more like the reality. And this experience, tough as it may be, is also a liberation. Being free of the cherished image which we can now see to be a mask, we are free to be the people we really are, and really want to be.

But this new sense of reality can be alarming. It may reveal things in our life that we were trying to avoid or evade. We might discover, for example, that we are far more alone in the world than we had wanted to admit, and more vulnerable to change and uncertainty. Our false self-image, and perhaps our sense of belonging to this or that group, had protected us somewhat from this difficult reality. With the freedom of a new self-awareness it can hit us forcibly. We may feel lost, confused or insecure. How do we connect with people and the world in a way that is truthful and honest, yet also safe? How do we connect with the reality that brought us into being, that can help us maybe make sense of this brief life of ours, and give some purpose to our life that will not be eroded by the knowledge that we all have to die? These are not simply questions about ourselves. They are about our relationship with the reality about us, and about the ultimate reality that makes our life possible. They are questions about God.

What 'God' means today

There are many ways of thinking and feeling about God, of

course. Today the variety is vast, and bewildering. But I am thinking of a very fundamental meaning of the word which we should all be able to recognize and accept. It is the sense of God as the ultimate reality of our life, whatever that might happen to be.[23] We are not referring to a particular being that we could imagine or describe, but to whatever reality it might be that lies behind or beneath all the particular realities we know of. To make sense of this idea we have to become aware of something in ourselves that points in that direction, possibly a *lack* of something we need but cannot identify, or a *longing* for something that could provide a basis or a meaning for our life. It is not so much a sense of God as that word is commonly understood, as a sense of 'a God-shaped hole'. I may have no idea what it is – it may even be a huge void or an absence - but I may have a very clear sense that without it, and without a positive relationship to it, my life is incomplete and unsatisfactory.

So 'God' in this sense is not an intellectual idea, an hypothesis, that answers a query about how the world works, or how the world began. It is a spiritual idea that answers our own inner longing for reality, our deep personal need for meaning and security and identity, but which nothing else – nothing in the world around us – seems to be able to answer.

So what might this reality be? That question seems to be inevitable once we have asked it, but it can cause us no end of trouble. It invites us to describe this final reality as we might describe anything else, and many descriptions have been offered. 'God is an infinite person', for example, 'essentially like us but on an infinite scale, unbounded in knowledge and power'. 'No,' says someone else, 'that is a contradiction. God cannot be infinite *and* personal. God has to be an *im*personal reality, if it is to be coherent and to explain how the universe exists. God has to be Energy or the Life Force or perhaps Being Itself'. 'But these are abstractions', says another eager intellectual. 'Better to think of God as simply the world personified. It's a human construction'. And finally, as in debates raging around us at the moment, someone says, 'This is pure speculation. There is no basis in fact for any of these ideas. It is pointless to believe in them and even possibly dangerous. So dismiss them, and stay with the simple facts of science'.

You see what has happened. A spiritual search has been turned into an intellectual inquiry. It is of course much easier to deal with this ultimate question of life if we debate ideas of what the ultimate reality might be. It is also very interesting. But we have to say it is evasive, and eventually unsatisfactory. The debate avoids and evades the question which lies at the base of it, the anxiety at being so alone or vulnerable in the world or the feeling of awe that the world exists at all. And that is often how we cope with anxiety and awe, is it not? Instead of exploring the feeling and finding what it might tell us about our situation in life, we grasp at something that seems to offer an immediate solution. 'Here is a revelation from God'. 'These are the facts of science'.

If there is a Quaker way of dealing with this question I would say that it is the advice to stay with the feeling, stay with the anxiety and awe. 'Be true to what you experience, and let the experience itself point the way through'. That is advice that Quakers too have to heed, I should say. Like others they too can grasp at ideas which seem to resolve a worry or a wonder, but which are not really grounded in experience. They can say, for example, that it is essential to believe in God as the ultimate power in the world and Quakerism is not thinkable without this belief, or they may say on the contrary – there is a minority of Quakers who do say this[24] – that it is important to believe that there is no God, and that such a belief is necessary for spiritual development. So, surprisingly perhaps, we have our own, quiet version of the God debate that is taking place in the world around us. I hope to show in what follows that people on both sides of the debate are rather missing the point.

Let me begin then by describing the distinctively Quaker approach to these things, elaborating on the Quaker advice about staying with the experience. And we need to note first of all a distinction between experience and belief.

The Quaker way avoids belief

Quakerism is perhaps unusual in this respect. Most religions or spiritualities set out their beliefs, their doctrines, as a necessary basis for pursuing the path. Quakers take the view that beliefs are not necessary, and may even be a hindrance. Quakers are serious about God, certainly, but they do not require belief in God as a starting point, or even as a goal to be aimed at. The question that concerns them is what helps you or hinders you in finding the reality that will enable you to live well. What you believe about the existence and nature of God may make little difference to how you live your life, or it may, if you adhere strongly to the belief, either way, actually prevent you from experiencing the reality of what you say you believe in.

Listen to these words of George Fox:

Silence all presumptuous talkers of God who see him not.[25]

I have translated this into modern English as follows:

You have the presumption to talk about God when you are not even aware of him? Silence, I tell you![26]

Most intellectuals of the time talked confidently of God, and often on the best authority, but Fox is telling them that if they have no real experience of God they cannot know what they are talking about, so had better shut up. In a tract from the early days – a tract not since published, incidentally – he tells us what he thinks is going on when people talk so confidently about God:

Silly man in his foolish imagination will go make an image of him... And you make images of God like yourselves... You poor silly creatures, empty of life or light or grace or truth which comes from the God of truth, to have your image makers make an image of him who the heaven of heavens is not able to contain... And yet you in your foolishness, darkness and ignorance go make an image of the incomprehensible God, and so you will comprehend him in the fashion of a man.[27]

To talk intelligibly about God when they have no direct experience of God, they have to use ideas and images which they (and others) are already familiar with. And it is somewhat reassuring to be able to tell people that God is essentially like them! So they create God in their own image. This is a remarkable insight for its time, anticipating an idea that was not to surface for another two hundred years: that, when faced with the void, humans project an image of themselves on to it, and so feel secure once again.

And listen to Samuel Fisher, a contemporary of Fox, but a quite learned man who became a Quaker after having studied theology at Oxford University (see Appendix 1 for a fuller text).

Query 1. What is God really in himself, without any definition?
Answer 1. God, as he is really in himself, is beyond all definition of ours at all... They only truly know him to be this or that, who witness him truly to be this or that to and within themselves. And those know him not... that prate this and that of him like [mag]pies and parrots, which may be taught... yet come not to find him and feel him so to be... in his own light, by which he draws nigh to, and is not far from every one of us. By which [light] ... in some measure, though not the same measure, he manifests something of himself in every

conscience.[28]

There are two things to note in these quotations.One is that God cannot be understood intellectually; it is folly and even arrogance to try to 'comprehend' God in this way, because God ends up looking and sounding like a human being. The other thing to note is that it is possible nevertheless to have a *sense or feeling* of God, which is somehow already in our conscience. Only people who open themselves to this experience can be said to *know* God, to 'see him', as Fox says. Those who merely talk of God, on the basis of what other people have said or written, are 'prating' like 'magpies and parrots'. They are mouthing what others have said, and stealing what others have produced. Margaret Fell came to realize that when George Fox first came to her church in Ulverston and spoke to the congregation after the minister had delivered his sermon:

When they had done singing, he stood up upon his seat or form and desired that he might have liberty to speak. And he that was in the pulpit said he might. And the first words that he spoke were as followeth: 'He is not a Jew that is one outward, neither is that circumcision which is outward, but he is a Jew that is one inward, and that is circumcision which is of the heart'. And so he went on and said, How that Christ was the Light of the world and lighteth every man that cometh into the world; and that by this Light they might be gathered to God, etc. And I stood up in my pew, and I wondered at his doctrine, for I had never heard such before. And then he went on, and opened the Scriptures, and said, 'The Scriptures were the prophets' words and Christ's and the apostles' words, and what as they spoke they enjoyed and possessed and had it from the Lord'. And said, 'Then what had any to do with the Scriptures, but as they came to the Spirit that gave them forth. You will say, Christ saith this, and the apostles say this; but what canst thou say? Art thou a child of Light and has walked in the Light, and what thou speakest is it inwardly from God?'

This opened me so that it cut me to the heart; and then I saw clearly we were all wrong. So I sat me down in my pew again, and cried bitterly. And I cried in my spirit to the Lord, 'We are all thieves, we are all thieves, we have taken the Scriptures in words and know nothing of them in ourselves'.[29]

How then are they supposed to know this truth for themselves, to gain this 'feeling' or 'sense' of God, as Fisher describes it? Fisher points us initially to something inside us, something apparently quite meagre: God 'manifests something of himself in every conscience'... But that will tell us only about ourselves, surely? Exactly. But that is where we have to begin.

Growing awareness

The experience of the light does not immediately bring us to an experience of God. It is initially a down-to-earth experience of ourselves, though drawing on an awareness that seems to come from outside ourselves. And it is where we need to begin, as the early Friends made quite clear. We cannot advance in our spiritual life until we have come to terms with our present experience of life. But when we do get a sense of ourselves as we are, we then begin to get a sense of God. Fox made that clear in an early tract, from about 1654, 'A word from the Lord to all the world':

So God Almighty open your understandings, all people every-where, that you may see yourselves. And if you take heed to that light which will exercise your consciences, it will let you see yourselves, which eye is the light, and this light will let you see God.[30]

That needs to be emphasized today because Friends sometimes have an easy way of speaking about God, which hasn't come to terms with the difficulty, the obstacle to our getting out of our egos. It is sometimes said that if we come to Meeting and sit in silence we can then experience God directly. This is what the German theologian Dietrich Bonhoeffer called 'cheap grace'. It doesn't of course happen like that, so Friends can get very disappointed and discouraged. But there is a Quaker way of looking for God, though it is sometimes dark and difficult, and if we follow that way we will surely experience what we feel we most need to know.

Moreover, when we do begin to get a sense of God we realize that it is quite different from what our previous idea of God might have led us to expect. This kind of reality will not fit into our ready-made concepts. And what started off perhaps as an intellectual quest will turn out to be something quite different. Yet the growing awareness that comes from waiting in the light will give us a new understanding which will help us to address those intellectual difficulties we might have started off with. Listen to Samuel Fisher again, that early Friend who had engaged in a serious intellectual quest before becoming a Quaker, and was therefore able to see how an intellectual quest could be resolved in experience:

Ye query, What God really is in himself? As God saith of himself [Exodus 3:14], 'I am that I am'... God is what he is; and if ye, who by your asking of us, profess yourselves to be yet ignorant of him... would know him in any measure as he really is in himself, my counsel to you is to stand still in his own counsel, namely, his light in your conscience, that in that you may be led forth into his life and likeness, even into the image of his son, the light of the world... Wait for his appearing in his own spirit and power to restore his own image in your hearts, that as he appeareth, ye may appear with him in glory, which is fullness of grace and truth, being transformed into his image from glory to glory, by the operation of his holy spirit, that as he appeareth ye may be like him, and so see him as he is.[31]

Fisher is saying in a more sophisticated way what Fox was saying earlier: when you really see yourselves you will then 'see God', not literally of course, but in the metaphorical sense of being aware of God. But Fisher is saying something more, which I think is very profound and very helpful to us, over three centuries later, with all our doubt and difficulty about the reality of God. He is telling us, not what God is like, what sort of a reality God is (which is impossible), but what we can do to get a deep sense and assurance of God. 'My counsel to you', he says, 'is to stand still in his counsel, namely his light in your consciences'. His advice to the doubters of his time is to refer them to the advice they are already being given in their consciences, if only they would listen to it. So they have to sit still, pay attention to what their conscience is telling them, whether good or bad, and let the light 'in the conscience' show them what is really going on in their life. What will this do for them? He is suggesting three things it will do for them:

1. It will make them more aware of themselves, and with such clarity and force that they will recognize it to be the truth. And this surprising discovery will then make them aware that something deep within them knows them better than they know themselves. This source of insight is so truthful, all-seeing and even compassionate, they will realize, that it has to come from God himself. So they become aware, as early Friends like to say, of 'that of God' within themselves, which assures them of an inner connection with God in themselves, even though in their everyday life they may be quite unaware of God.

2. The second thing this practice will do for them is inspire them to live more in harmony with this truth and love they have found within them. They will recognize their normal way of life as relatively selfish and uncaring, but this inner light is so affirming and liberating, when it is taken seriously, that they will want to make *that* the centre of their lives. This inner source will become their true self, gradually maybe, but inevitably. In other words, they will become more godlike. I don't say - and Friends have never said – they will become God. They remain human, after all, and God is not human. So they find another language to speak about this experience. They grow 'into the image of God', as Fisher says; 'that you may be led forth into his life and likeness, even into the image of his son'. According to the Book of Genesis, you will remember, human beings, unlike the other creatures, were 'created in the image and likeness of God' (1:26f). They are being compared to children who bear the likeness of their parents. So humans were made to reflect the invisible and infinite reality of God on the visible and finite plane of this world. This great potential, the story goes, was frustrated and blocked by humans' failure to become aware of this and to see any point to their lives beyond their individual selves. Early Friends picked up this idea, though, believing that that extraordinary potential to become godlike had been released again, just as it had previously in the time of Jesus. The 'image of God' in humans was being wonderfully restored. This of course was not a doctrine that Friends taught on the basis of the Bible, but a testimony to their own experience of being inwardly restored, using the language of the Bible to describe it.

3. This then led to the third thing that the practice would do for them. Becoming godlike, as they lived from that

something of God within them, they would develop a sense of connection with God and therefore a sense of what God really was. They would 'see God', as Fox says: 'As he appeareth' – in their quiet meditation and worship, Fisher implies – 'ye may be like him, and so see him as he is'. (Cf. 1 John 3:1-3, where the same phrases are used, but in the reverse order).Notice the little word 'so'. You will grow to be like him, and *so* you will see him as he is. The idea behind this, again, is that of children 'made in the image and likeness' of their parents. As they grow up, they get to become like their parents – at least as they knew them when young. And as they become more like them, they get to understand who their parents were, and are. So Fisher is saying to his readers: Because your own divine self has come to life, you will know intuitively, from experience, what God is. It still cannot be described rationally, because it goes beyond the world of people and things that our reason is designed to cope with. They will be confident in their knowledge nonetheless, because they are intimately aware of it, rather as they are intimately aware of themselves and those whom they love.

Speaking of God

The first advice, then, is to follow the advice we are already being given in our conscience. It is an invitation to explore the possibilities of our own present experience of life, including our negative experiences of anxiety, guilt and uncertainty. There is also a promise that if we venture on the path we will discover the huge positive of awareness and faith. Would it help to evoke that experience if we were to try and describe it? Possibly. There is a risk that any such description might be taken as a belief, an idea that could be detached from the experience and regarded as true in itself. It would then defeat its purpose. But if it is taken as an expression or interpretation of the experience, it could indeed be helpful. We Quakers have a word for such talk, as we shall see later on. It is 'testimony'. Our talk about God and other mysteries of life has the character of 'testifying' to our experience of these things.

So any description we offer has to be accompanied by a health warning. Here is one such warning from a Quaker of the eighteenth century, Anthony Benezet, who was best known for his pioneering work against slavery. He may have been thinking about this work when he wrote this entry to his Notebook, wondering why so many right-thinking Christians were so insensitive to the plight of the African slaves and the injustice being done to them:

> I know some think great advantage will arise from people's having what are called right ideas of God; and that those opinions are productive of much tenderness and charity in the minds of such who adopt them; but has this indeed been the case? Have the meekness and gentleness of Christ been more apparent in those who have been zealous advocates for this opinion than in other people? Ideas, however exalted they may appear, except impressed on the mind by truth, are still but bare ideas, and can have no influence in subduing that love of the world, that carnality of mind, that obduracy of heart, and principally that poisonous idolatry of self, so apt, under one subtle form or another, to insinuate itself even into the hearts of such as have already made some good advances in religion.[32]

William Penn, a century before, was similarly sceptical about 'right ideas of God'. Behind such ideas, he could see, was the mistaken idea that Truth could finally be established in a set of words. Words were not fitted for this purpose. To get to the truth we had to let go of words and learn a different language, a 'language of spirit'. But having heard that language, we might

after all be able to say something about it in human words, as
Penn does here, in his aphoristic sayings on our knowledge of
God:

508. Words are for others, not for ourselves. Nor for God, who
     hears not as bodies do, but as spirits should.
509. If we would know this dialect, we must learn of the divine
     principle in us. As we hear the dictates of that, so God hears
     us.
510. There we may see him too in all his attributes – though but
     in little, yet as much as we can apprehend or bear, for as he
     is in himself he is incomprehensible, and dwelleth in that
     light which no eye can approach. But in his image we may
     behold his glory, enough to exalt our apprehensions of God
     and to instruct us in that worship which pleaseth him.
511. Men may tire themselves in a labyrinth of search and talk of
     God, but if we would know him indeed, it must be from the
     impressions we receive of him; and the softer our hearts are,
     the deeper and livelier those will be upon us.
512. If he has made us sensible of his justice by his reproof, of his
     patience by his forbearance, of his mercy by his forgiveness,
     of his holiness by the sanctification of our hearts through his
     spirit, we have a grounded knowledge of God. This is
     experience, that speculation; this enjoyment, that report. In
     short, this is undeniable evidence with the realities of
     religion, and will stand all winds and weathers.[33]

The implication of these sayings is that we could, after all, say
something about God if we related it specifically to our
experience. The first experience may be awe at the reality that far
surpasses our understanding, yet at the same time somehow
undergirds everything. So God can be described negatively as
'incomprehensible', dwelling 'in that light that no eye can
approach' (510). But in the dim reflected image of his glory – in a

dull mirror, perhaps, that doesn't reflect the full brightness[34] - we can see something that we can just understand and appreciate. The mirror, of course, ('the glass') is in 'our hearts' (511), the very centre of our being. As our hearts are moved and changed by being opened to 'the divine principle in us', we gain knowledge of what God is and does. As we look honestly at our lives in silent waiting we become more clearly aware of what is right and wrong in our lives. This is already an experience of God's 'justice', Penn says, as well as God's truth. As we accept this judgement on our life we experience acceptance ourselves, 'forgiveness', which is an experience of God's mercy, and so on. Here, says Penn confidently, 'we have a grounded knowledge of God' (512). We can say on the basis of this more positive experience that God is all-knowing, truthful, just and forgiving.

We could summarize our discussion so far by saying that we gain a sense of God first by becoming aware of a depth in ourselves that connects us with something beyond the range of our ego and ego-based concepts – 'that of God' within us – and secondly by experiencing the transformation that takes place when we open ourselves to what this deep self will reveal to us. We see ourselves as we are, broken and conflicted, yet find ourselves being healed and restored as we accept this truth about ourselves, not immediately perhaps, but surely and steadily as we continue to open ourselves to reality. We are not sure how all this happens, but we are confident that some reality in and around us knows very well what is going on and cares sufficiently to mend us and make us whole. We have to say this, if we are honest, because when we faced reality – at last – we found it didn't hurt. On the contrary we have been made happy and whole by it. The experience of being made whole by opening ourselves to the truth conveys a deep message to us: ultimately reality is loving.

So much is 'well-grounded knowledge'. But can we say more than that? Can we say more about this 'reality in and around us' that does such remarkable things? What kind of a reality could it be? It does personal things like revealing and reproving and forgiving, but it has no bodily form in space and time so it cannot be described as a person. We can speak poetically of this reality, of course, avoiding literal language, and this is mostly how Quakers do speak of it. However confident they may be to speak of God's love or power, they will usually indicate as well that this love or power is elusive, and not what we normally understand by the word. That is, they are using words in an unusual way: not literally to describe this reality, but metaphorically to hint at it, point towards it, or perhaps to evoke a sense of it.

This is half of an answer. It answers the *how* but not the *what*. If our language about God is a matter of pointing, not describing, it has to point *to* something, or *towards* it. What is this? Are Quakers perhaps fudging the issue when they decline to give a definition of God, but imply nonetheless that there is something out there that answers to the name? I would have to agree that for many Quakers this is true. But I would have to say also that in this respect they have not grasped how radical the Quaker vision is, how serious it is about letting go of beliefs and words, and trusting to the experience that comes through silence. So the way to deal with this question of what it is we point to in our God-language is to look, again, at the experience out of which it arises. I will draw now more on my own experience, and invite you to reflect on yours.

Pointing beyond

Let us look in particular at the experience that gives us a sense of a reality beyond what we can grasp. It is an experience, as I have said, in which we get out of our egos. This may happen spontaneously and unexpectedly, or it may happen in the practice of meditation, of waiting consciously 'in the light'. In one way or another, the ego, which is the usual centre and point of reference for our life, gives up its assertiveness, its demand, and gives way to what is happening around it. It becomes a passive observer. As a result, it is more able to see clearly and feel directly. Moreover, it gives way to a deeper capacity for awareness which can see things as they are and see them whole. This insight, as we have seen, can be hugely important for individuals, who now gain a sense of what they themselves really are. But it is significant in another way: it gives them a new sense of the world, and a new feeling for it. Whereas before they would have thought of the world as something other than themselves, the sum total of everything they had to deal with in life, the reality 'out there' in contrast to the personal reality 'in here', now they have come to see that ultimately there is no separation. They and the world are one thing. For practical purposes they need to keep some sense of being apart, some sense of their individuality, but that now has no ultimate significance. The idea that they were alone in the world, struggling to survive in an ultimately indifferent world, was an illusion. Both they and the world were being misconstrued because of a fundamental ignorance of who they were.

This means that reality as a whole can be seen and felt as a whole, and 'I' and 'you' and 'they' are all part of it. Everything is included and interconnected. No one part of it is superior, ultimate, definitive, or basic. The whole sustains itself, or perhaps we should say, it is sustained, because no one process that we humans can identify could possibly account for the whole. Our various scientific and personal explanations of things all have their place, but they have their place in a totality we none of us can comprehend. Reality is finally mysterious.

Our little word 'God' tries to name that mystery. And it is important that it does. It indicates that our world is all of a piece, grounded in and held together by a reality beyond our grasp, but which is nonetheless felt as the basis of our own individual lives. It points to what transcends our world, unites it and sustains it in being. It points but it does not describe. It offers no concepts or images that enable us to grasp the reality in our minds. It can only invite us to look and to see for ourselves. And that, as we have observed, means looking initially *into* ourselves so that we can eventually see everything differently.

There is also the possibility of *feeling* things differently. We can respond to the 'promptings of love' as well as 'of truth'. Indeed one seems to follow the other. When I see that I am not fundamentally separate from other people, for example, I can feel a new closeness to them. If I can then affirm this closeness by caring for them, I express a love that goes well beyond my usual, ego-centred desire. This is the spiritual meaning of love. It is loving regardless of family or tribal ties, regardless of calculated profit or advantage, and regardless of how others may judge me. There is no calculation at all, only action in response to a feeling for others, a desire to help, based on the insight of our fundamental oneness. But this love generates an insight of its own. Loving another person in this way enables us to share in that mysterious activity that makes the world what it is. Loving another is affirming the whole and therefore participating in the making of it. It is 'growing into the image of God' as creator of the world and '*so* seeing him as he is'. Love in this sense is an experience of God.

The significance in everyday life

Such experiences of God can be immensely significant to us, even though we are unable to put them into words. They give *a sense of the ultimate reality of our life*, the ultimate context in which our life has to be lived. With such an experience we *know*. We don't have to believe. We know that we are grounded in what's real, that we are connected and not ultimately alone, that we belong and are in some sense secure. This confidence takes the anxiety out of life. We are limited, of course, just as before, and our life is as uncertain as ever, but we find that we are able to accept this as part of what life is. We live and we die, and it's all a gift:

Naked I came from the womb,
naked I shall return whence I came.
The Lord gives and The Lord takes away;
blessed be the name of the Lord.[35]

It has significance too in *enabling us to trust* reality when things go hard for us, knowing that our acceptance of what happens, whatever happens, will enable us to respond creatively. And it enables us to trust the deeper impulses and insights of our life that emerge especially as we sit in silent waiting. This is the point of our first Advice, as quoted before:

Take heed, dear Friends, to the prompting of love and truth in your hearts. Trust them as the leadings of God...

Trusting is important when these experiences are only fleeting and momentary, as they usually are. We may have only one such experience in a lifetime, but it could be enough to ground our confidence in God and God's leadings in our day-to-day living.

Such an experience may also *help that intellectual quandary* that afflicts many of us about what the ultimate reality is, and whether there really is such a thing. When we experience God in this existential way, that is, as part of our awareness of life as we live it, we can't think of it as some kind of an object or thing, or even a person. God is not something or someone that might not exist. God is not out there, and God is not *not* out there. God is everywhere and nowhere, another dimension, if you like, to life and the world as we know them. This is already beginning to sound like nonsense, I know, but that's a useful reminder that we very soon get to the limit of words, and of logic, when we try to describe the experience of reality in this direct and fundamental way.

If we could hold on to this personal way of talking about God, I don't think we would have such problems about the question of whether God exists. We can let that question go, as irrelevant. We will still have differences of language, of course, and some people may still be uncomfortable about using the word 'God', with all its heavy associations. They will find other ways to express themselves and not go unheard, so they will feel free to hear others who still find that word evocative and powerful.

The purpose of words in our spiritual life, as Isaac Penington once memorably put it, 'is to bring men [and women] to the knowledge of things beyond what words can utter'.[36]

Chapter three

Meeting Others

I emphasized in the last chapter that the 'Quaker way of looking for God' involves a personal process of transformation. It cannot be otherwise, given the Quaker rejection of external things as the means of finding God. Each person has to find the truth for themselves, and each person is able to do this because they each have something of God in them. It may be unknown to them, unrecognised or disregarded, but as soon as they begin to pay it attention it will begin to show itself and show something of their life as well. It is there in the conscience, nudging them on the things they do right and wrong, so they have only to notice and acknowledge it and they will be able to see things in a different light. They will be on a spiritual journey.

Does this mean that the Quaker journey is essentially an individual one? You might think so, from what I have said so far. But I have wanted to emphasize the individual path because it has been so much neglected in present day Quakerism, which tends to see the Meeting for Worship as the whole basis and focus of our spiritual life. When we have seen what we are each called to do individually, however, we will be in a position to recognize that the Quaker path also involves others. There are many spiritualities that emphasize the individual almost exclusively, and some of the new spiritualities suggest that each person has to find the particular truth that suits them. But this is not the Quaker way, however much we might learn from other spiritualities. The Meeting of Friends was always important, right from the beginning, especially the Meeting for Worship. Early Friends met together even if they had to travel great distances, even if they were forbidden by law to meet outside the walls of the established church. Why was this? There were a number of reasons. Let's begin with the simplest.

Sharing with one another

Early Friends needed one another in order to survive. Anyone who rejected the parish church and refused to attend services or pay tithes was out on their ear. They would no longer be supported by the parish system. No burials, marriages or even births – at least none that would have been given some public recognition. Perhaps no employment either. Many thousands of people found themselves in this position in the mid-seventeenth century, mostly as a matter of conscience. In the North West of England there was a particularly large number of them, and many of them banded together for mutual support and silent worship, waiting for a new prophet or teacher to show them the way. These were the Seekers whom Fox met when he first came to these parts in 1652. He refused to be their teacher, but he did point the way for them each to find a teacher within themselves. And he urged them at the same time to band together, as they had done, to support one another in any practical way that was needed. 'Tender to one another in all convenient outward things, for that is the least love'.[37] Our practical needs may not be so urgent as theirs, with our modern support systems, but practical help is still needed, and it still binds us together. We also need one another socially, perhaps even more now than they did then. Our society is more fragmented and alienated than theirs. Our modern technology, our greater mobility, our determination as individuals to make a life for ourselves – these have all contrived to pull us somewhat apart from one another. We therefore feel more isolated individually and feel a strong need to connect with other people who will have at least some sympathy with us and some understanding of our particular concerns. We sense, rightly, that we cannot be fulfilled in our lives if we cannot share our lives with others, and believe we participate in something much larger than ourselves.[38]

But there is a more pressing need: to connect with others spiritually:

We need others to mirror back how they see us and to affirm us. Exposure to the light means we have to see ourselves as we are, to strip ourselves 'naked', as Early Friends liked to say, and this, as we have seen, can be a difficult experience. Others can help us in this by reflecting back how they see us, and by accepting us as we are. There is no room for pretence here. On the contrary, the kind of affirmation and acceptance that each of us needs can only be received when we are completely open with one another about how we are. This is given practical expression in the way we sit together in Meeting. We sit facing one another. We do not face an altar or pulpit or image, as if what connected us spiritually was something outside us. We are looking to each other and the secret interchange that occurs when we look at one another fact to face. Friends have made a point of this even for larger gatherings. They described their first Yearly Meeting in London as follows:

> We did conclude among ourselves to settle a meeting, to see one another's faces, and open our hearts one to another in the truth of God once a year, as formerly it used to be.[39]

The presence of the other is then included in our meditation. Indeed the face of the other in front of me may challenge me to 'face up to' myself, my real self, or comfort me in the knowledge that I am accepted as I am.[40] This affirmation by others will help us in turn to affirm and accept ourselves, whatever it is in ourselves that we might feel to be unacceptable. And if we accept *ourselves* as we are, we are more able to accept others, without judgment or suspicion. Fox has two good bits of advice on this to Meetings:

Mind that which first convinced you, that power of God which first awakened you, and arise and live in it, that all your eyes, minds and hearts may be kept single and naked to God [i.e. honest and sincere], and to one another, unclothed of all that is contrary.[41]

Being written all in one another's hearts, have all one voice and the pure language of truth, where in all plainness of speech things may be spoken in nakedness of heart one unto another in the eternal unity of the one spirit.[42]

This is not how people normally behave in groups, it has to be said, or even in families. It seems too risky and trusting. But Friends have recognized that such honesty and openness can lead to a deep sharing of our lives that brings insight and strength to all of us. The advice is echoed in our current Book of Discipline:

It is our search for God's way that has drawn us together. In our meeting we can each hope to find love, support, challenge, practical help and a sense of belonging. We should *bring ourselves as we are*, whatever our age, our strength, our weakness; and be able to share friendship and warmth.[43]

This openness becomes possible when we realize that we are heard and accepted, when we 'find love', as the Book of Discipline says, meaning a warm acceptance. This is what Patricia Loring calls 'a listening spirituality'[44]. It seems to be the condition for another piece of advice in the Book, following George Fox:

Friends, meet together and know one another in that which is eternal, which was before the world was.[45]

'That which is eternal' is that deep part of each of us which links us to God, the Eternal, and which we can get to only when we let go of the image we have of ourselves and see the truth of what we are. As we are each able to do this we 'meet' and 'know one another' in a quite different way.

We each have a limited understanding and need one another to share our insights. All our resources are limited, of course, but this is also true of that special divine source we each have buried within us. We each have a 'measure' of the light, as Early Friends used to say. Remember Samuel Fisher's words that I quoted before:

> By which light... in some measure, though not the same measure, he manifests something of himself in every conscience.[46]

Fox had to remind a meeting of women Friends that they should not expect everyone to have the same insight, so that it was the responsibility of those with better understanding to help those with less:

> Now when the women are met together in the light and in the gospel, the power of God, some are of a more large capacity and understanding than other women, and are able to inform and instruct and stir up others into diligence, virtue and righteousness... and to help them that be of weaker capacities and understandings in the wisdom of God, that they may be fruitful in every good work and word.[47]

It is perhaps surprising that this recognition of different abilities did not lead Friends to adopt the practice of other churches and 'ordain' certain people to 'the ministry'. (Something like this did happen later in America, in fact.[48]) But they were averse to setting certain people above others, so as not to lose the benefit of all participating. Some who are 'weak in understanding' may be strong in something else, like practical help or ability to listen. The 'ministry' is then mutual, and the community grows, as everyone gains confidence in themselves to give what they can, and confidence in others to give what they need. This brings us to the next point.

We have different gifts. So we are greatly enriched by the variety of gifts in a group. Women too, says Fox – against those who wanted to limit their service – are 'stewards of the manifold grace of God'.[49] And all these 'manifold' gifts are found to be necessary, which is another reason for not setting some apart as 'holy':

> Are there not different states, different degrees, different growths, different places?... Therefore, watch every one to feel and know his own place and service in the body, and to be sensible of the gifts, places, and services of others, that the Lord may be honoured in all, and every one owned and honoured in the Lord, and no otherwise.[50]

This is acknowledged in *Quaker Faith and Practice:*

> We recognize a variety of ministries. In our worship these include those who speak under the guidance of the Spirit, and those who receive and uphold the work of the Spirit in silence and prayer. We also recognise as ministry service on our many committees, hospitality and childcare, the care of finance and premises, and many other tasks. We value those whose ministry is not in an appointed task but is in teaching, counselling, listening, prayer, enabling the service of others, or other service in the meeting or the world.[51]

Out of this openness and sharing comes an experience of unity. The old facades are down, our fear of criticism or rejection, so we are able to be ourselves and to accept others as they are. We find unity in our common humanity; but also – and this is slightly different – in the Spirit. We know now that we belong together, that we can trust one another and that we can do things together we would never be able to do apart. Out of this knowledge comes strength, comfort, love and confidence to act.

This is not a unity we have to create by artfully establishing common interests. It is already there, if we have the eyes to see it. The point is that, waiting in the light, we do see it; we lose our customary selfish viewpoint and see others as they are, without distortion:

> All they that are in the light are in unity; for the light is but one.[52]

Holding together

For all this, we still have our differences and problems. Fox recognized this too, despite the optimistic words I have just quoted. A little later in that paper he describes how unity actually comes about, although now he is talking not about 'the light' but about 'the word', which may be confusing, though Fox often does equate the two:[53]

> This is a word of reconciliation, that reconcileth together to God, and gathers the hearts of his together, to live in love and unity one with another, and lets them see how they have been strangers and aliens from the life of God... Abiding inwardly in the light, it will let you see one another and the unity one with another.[54]

How do we achieve this, given that we have no priests or doctrines to bring obedience or conformity? The Quaker answer – one of Fox's many original ideas – is 'gospel order'. That is an order or discipline in a community brought about, not by the imposition of rules or correct beliefs, but by the acceptance of each member of the light within. This is what is meant by 'the gospel' here, which is not understood as a public message, as with other churches, but as the message each of us hears in our hearts about what is true and right.[55] In practice that requires a discipline of waiting in silence until we each become aware of the issue before us, and by sharing our insights can learn what now needs to be done. (We shall see the implications of this in the next chapter when we consider 'the Quaker way of making decisions'.) If there is a conflict in the meeting, which is bound to happen from time to time, we try to get to the truth of the matter, without pushing or defending our individual or factional interest. That takes quite a bit of discipline! But the Quaker experience is that it works. When we are still and quiet, we can let go our anxious sense of self and see the needs and interests of others more clearly. And when we all do this, sitting together, we can discern what is objectively right for all of us. That is what early Friends meant by 'abiding in the truth'. The truth, of course is not always welcome, and Friends can be as prone as anyone to turn away from the truth to the comfort of their own opinion. Then, sooner or later, there will be a clash of opinions and Friends will either struggle with a conflict to which they can see no obvious resolution, or retreat further into their shells and do everything they can to avoid further clashes. The conflict of course continues, but unseen, gnawing away at the life and unity of the meeting.[56] They may then need help from outside, to come back to the truth they have been avoiding and to open up their hearts to what has really been going on. But the sooner they face the situation the better. If someone is angry or upset in a meeting, for example, the first thing to do is to discover why this is, in an empathetic way, and to deal with the issue as it arises. If others have been hurt or affected by it in any way, they too should be heard, with an open heart, then gradually the truth will emerge and Friends will have the opportunity to see it together and to embrace it. That is the way that 'reconciliation' can be achieved, as George Fox described it, and that is the way the meeting will rediscover its unity.

It is possible that after a generation or two the early Friends lost their confidence in this process, and therefore their commitment to it. They had mostly been brought up as Friends and had not experienced the huge discovery of the first Friends. The dynamic practice became a matter of form, ironically. The Meeting would discuss every detail of Friends' lives, from how they dressed to who they married, agree a Minute on the subject, and the Minute would then become a rule for everyone to follow. A century or so later Friends rebelled against this rigidity, but they never quite recovered the dynamism of early Friends. Now that we know a little more about those beginnings, we have a chance to recover the openness and spontaneity of those first Quaker meetings. The unity that Friends aim at is, after all, quite natural and easy. It arises from our own, deeper nature, as soon as that is allowed to express itself. When it happens it is like a good, well-functioning family. And Fox proposed just this as a goal for each Meeting:

Keep up your meetings for worship, and your men and women's meetings for the affairs of truth, both Monthly and Quarterly. And, after you are settled, you may join together and build a meeting house. And do not strive about outward things; but dwell in the love of God, for that will unite you together, and make you kind and gentle one towards another; and to seek one another's good and welfare, and to be helpful one to another; and see that nothing be lacking among you, then all will be well. And let temperance and patience and kindness and brotherly love be exercised among you, so that you may abound in virtue, and the true humility; living in peace, showing forth the nature of Christianity, that you may all live as a family.[57]

So Quaker spiritual practice reflects the fact that humans are social animals, that much of their disorientation and dysfunction arises from conflicts in community, and that in seeking to remedy the human condition we have to begin with ourselves and our human relationships.

Worshipping together

I have kept this till last, not because I think it less important, but to get it into clearer perspective. Our practice of coming together once a week to sit in silence makes sense only if we have learned to do that during the week and have got to know the people we sit with in ordinary, everyday interactions. This would have been easier perhaps for the first Friends, since silence was part of their lives anyway, and the people with whom they worshipped would have met in other ways during the week. When they came together on Sunday, or whenever, they would truly 'meet' one another, since they knew one another well from their daily contacts, and they would be spiritually 'trained' to be open to one another and the experience of corporate worship. The worshipping group wouldn't have to carry the whole burden of their individual spiritual lives, and the meeting for worship would not, by itself, have to sustain them for the rest of the week. Nevertheless, the gathering together was always special. We can see this best when we recognize that, initially at least, they would be doing the same thing together as they did on their own or in their families.

What was the same?

We have some clear directions from Alexander Parker, writing a letter to Friends in 1660:

> The first that enters into the place of your meeting... turn in thy mind to the light, and wait upon God singly, as if none were present but the Lord; and here thou art strong. Then the

next that comes in, let them in simplicity of heart sit down and turn in to the same light, and wait in the spirit; and so all the rest coming in, in the fear of the Lord, sit down in pure stillness and silence of all flesh, and wait in the light... Those who are brought to a pure still waiting upon God in the spirit, are come nearer to the Lord than words are; for God is a spirit, and in the spirit is he worshipped... In such a meeting there will be an unwillingness to part asunder, being ready to say in yourselves, it is good to be here: and this is the end of all words and writings to bring people to the eternal living Word.[58]

This corresponds to the direction given to individuals who wanted to find the reality of religion and to experience its liberating and life-giving power for themselves. They were to become still and silent, so that their normal anxious thoughts would subside, and then to turn their minds to the truth that their conscience was alerting them to. If they faced that truth and accepted it, they would find greater truth, and that would enable them to see who they really were and how they could now live freely and fruitfully. That was the process. And when they came together to worship they would first have to check with their conscience to see if there was anything in their life that needed dealing with before they could open themselves genuinely to the needs of others. Even then, the point of the exercise in being together was to become more fully aware of the truth of their lives and to respond inwardly to what was revealed to them:

They must be in it [the spirit], and in the truth, to worship the God of all truth.[59]

Everyone is to be in it [the truth] and to walk in the truth, and in the spirit, and to come to the truth in their own particulars [their own individual experience]... And so none can worship the God of truth, but who come to the truth in their own hearts.[60]

What was different?

The first thing is that we come to feel part of the group, not isolated or alone. This is a good experience in itself, but it can lead to something even better, a sense of being united in the spirit, held together by something larger than ourselves, which can nourish us and enlighten us as a group. Perhaps the best account of this experience was given in Robert Barclay's *Apology*, chapter 11, back in 1676, the first systematic defence of the Quaker practice. Here's one small part of it:

> Meeting together not only outwardly in one place, but thus inwardly in one spirit, and in one 'name of Jesus' (which is his power and virtue), they come thereby to enjoy and feel the arisings of this life, which, as it prevails in each particular [individual], becomes as a flood of refreshment, and overspreads the whole meeting.[61]

But to get to this experience we have to become aware of the people we are with, and maybe to get a sense of how they are. Fox did not give very much advice about Meeting for Worship, surprisingly perhaps, but in one letter he gave some searching advice about how to settle down and tune in to the others. The letter was directed mostly to Friends who had been travelling around the country, debating the Quaker cause, and might have got quite heated in their confrontation with Puritan opponents:

> Friends, be watchful and careful in all meetings ye come into. When a man is come newly out of the world he cometh out of the dirt. Then he must not be rash. For now when he cometh into a silent meeting, that is another state. Then he must come and feel his own spirit how it is, when he cometh to those that

sit silent; for he may come in the heat of his spirit out of the world [whereas the others are still and cool]... Friends, come into that which is over all the spirits of the world, with that ye may see where others stand, and reach that which is of God in everyone.[62]

You see that Fox is advising them to deal with their own personal stuff first of all, so that they can then be free to open themselves to the others, to 'see where others stand'. But it also suggests a down-to-earth approach to the meeting as a whole: just become aware of who is there and how they are. When we have done that we can consider what might concern us as a group. Are there issues of disharmony, anxiety or practical concern? This is not the time to think about them, but a time to hold them in the light, and hold the Meeting in the light. See the relevance of that old Quaker phrase. 'Holding' is not *doing* anything with it, not yet, it is just taking notice, absorbing what is really going on, feeling the joy or the pain of it. It might be like holding a wounded bird in our hands, or a newly found precious stone. It is a rather unique way of seeking the truth. I heard an ecologist once describe how he would get to know a new ecological environment, a river or a forest or just a field that was unfamiliar to him. He would sit in the field, or by the river, in silence, still and attentive, watching everything that was going on, and he would stay there for hours, until eventually he had a sense of the whole place and the life of that place. That seems to me like a Meeting for Worship.

We are coming together, finally, to 'worship'. That is not something we can plan, or organize, or even consciously undertake. As with our experience of unity in the group, it is a response of the heart to what we are made aware of when we sit in silent waiting.

Worship is our response to an awareness of God. We can

worship alone, but when we join with others in expectant waiting we may discover a deeper sense of God's presence.[63]

We may become aware as we sit together that we are part of a greater unity, a unity of life, perhaps, or a unity of being. Alternatively, we may become aware that the ministry that is being spoken in Meeting comes, not just from the person speaking, but from something deep inside them which is also inside us, because what is being said speaks to us directly and exactly. Or, we may become aware that the truth we are discerning, through both the ministry and the silent meditation, is part of the ultimate truth we have always been longing for. We may not understand what it is we are experiencing here, but we can be sure we are experiencing something beyond our normal selves and the normal world we inhabit. It may fill us with awe, or wonder or gratitude. And if we give ourselves to that feeling, and say 'yes' to it, that is surely true worship.

Part of the response may be to stand up in the Meeting and speak. This is 'ministry', in our current Quaker language. Another response may be to recognize that we have to settle a difference with someone or to help sort out a social problem. This is a 'leading'. If the leading continues and grows so that we feel led to devote some part of our life to it, it becomes a 'concern', which others also might join in, in which case it becomes a 'concern of the Meeting'.

Worship, ministry, leading, concern– these are all produced from within us, whether individually or collectively, but not from our conscious mind. We cannot *do* them, only respond consciously to what is being given or shown us. But we can consciously take care of the conditions that make the process possible. We can provide a building that is suitable for quiet waiting together, and yet obviously open for anyone to join. We can fix a good time to meet, and arrange other meetings for learning and support and planned action. These are our responsibility. We also appoint clerk, elders and overseers to ensure that the Meeting can do its business and care for its members. But these too, as we shall see in the next chapter, are also dependent on being 'led', i.e. they require us to care unselfishly for others and to discern the right thing to be done, and that can only come, finally, from the spirit in all of us.

Chapter four

Making Decisions

After looking at our general approach to spirituality in the previous chapters, I want to look now at something rather specific: the Quaker way of making decisions. In particular, we will look at the Meeting for Business, leaving till the next chapter our consideration of decisions and choices in personal life. Meeting for Business may seem relatively humdrum, but, as we shall see when we look at it in detail, it gives a surprisingly clear demonstration of what Quakerism itself is about. It is of course a subtle and sometimes difficult process that we go through, so it is not easy at first to understand. We have been recently helped in this by two books that describe it well, one from inside the Society of Friends, Barry Morley's *Beyond Consensus,* and one from outside, Michael Sheeran's *Beyond Majority Rule.* Sheeran, a Catholic, is surprised at the effectiveness of our method, for all its apparent idealism, and he sees it as unique in the modern world. All the more surprising, then, that such a subtle and unusual practice has survived all these years. (In Sheeran's own order, the Jesuits, there was a similar practice of discernment in the beginning but it has apparently not survived. He made this study of the Quakers to see how the original practice might be recovered.)

Our method of making decisions together is probably the practice we have best preserved from early times. The individual practice of meditation, which I described in the first chapter, has largely gone into abeyance, but our corporate practice of deciding things together has remarkably survived intact. We can get a sense of this continuity by listening to a description of the early practice by one of the leaders of that time, Edward Burrough. He was born and bred in Underbarrow near Kendal in the North

West of England, but spent most of his life travelling for Friends, leading the first mission in London in 1654, lobbying parliament, writing pamphlets, then dying all too early from his treatment in Newgate Prison. He wrote a pamphlet in 1662 about those first meetings, and contrasted them with meetings of other people he knew from that time, from the New Model Army under Cromwell to the churches that were then struggling to shape the life of England:

> We therefore... did... ordain and appoint that the men Friends of the City (not excluding any) should meet together at the Bull and Mouth[64] or elsewhere once in the fortnight, or once a month, as they in the wisdom of God should find it necessary, for the management of truth's affairs... that they should order in outward things relating to truth, and be assisting one to another, for the good and honour and service of the truth, and the Friends of it, so much as in them lay, according to that measure of the wisdom of God given to them, in perfect love and unity together, bearing one another's burdens, and helping together in mutual accord and good will...
>
> Thus for these causes, and for these ends,... was your meeting of men as aforesaid ordained and appointed...[65]
>
> Being orderly come together, not to spend time with needless, unnecessary and fruitless discourses, but to proceed in the wisdom of God... to hear and consider... not in the way of the world, as a worldly assembly of men, by hot contest, by seeking to out-speak and over-reach one another in discourse, as if it were controversy between party and party of men, or two sides violently striving for dominion, in the way of carrying on some worldly interest for self-advantage; not deciding affairs by the greater vote, or the number of men, as the world, who have not the wisdom and power of God... But in the wisdom, love and fellowship of God, in gravity,

patience, meekness, in unity and concord, submitting one to another in lowliness of heart, and in the holy spirit of truth and righteousness, all things to be carried on; by hearing and determining every matter coming before you in love, coolness, gentleness and dear unity. I say, as only one party, all for the truth of Christ... to determine of things by a general mutual accord, in assenting together as the one man in the spirit of truth and equity, and by the authority thereof[66].

If you read the section in our current *Faith and Practice* on 'The Sense of the Meeting' (3.02- 3.07), you will see how close we are today to what Burrough described. (See Appendix 2).

I need to add something to Burrough's description, though, or rather draw out something that was stated only implicitly. It is in that phrase, which Burrough repeats four times, 'in the wisdom of God'. This is saying that Friends do not rely on their own wisdom, however good that might be. They are looking for something beyond themselves, though it comes, when it does come, *through* them. That is the significance of Barry Morley's title, *Beyond Consensus*, and it is the point he most wants to make. We bring our minds to the issues we think about, certainly, but we do not resolve the issues simply by bringing our minds to them. We wait to be enlightened. Morley therefore contrasts this spiritual way with the more rational way of 'consensus'. Consensus is achieved through:

a process of reasoning in which reasonable people search for a satisfactory decision... Through consensus we decide it; through [a] sense of the meeting we turn it over, allowing it to be decided. 'Reaching a consensus is a secular process', says a Friend. 'In sense of the meeting God gets a voice'.[67]

This process can take a long time, of course. Who knows when we will all be enlightened so that we can all agree what needs to be done? It might prove to be difficult and even trying if everyone has to get on board, including the stubborn ones and the dull ones. So why do we do it this way?

Why this distinctive practice?

The first point to make is that while other ways of making a decision may be quicker, they may not result in a better decision. If the decision is made by someone in authority or by an appointed committee, it may not coincide with what most people want or think. If it is made by a public debate in which the issue is thought through from both sides, it might still miss the real point. Reason, thought and debate are very useful and often fair, but they are also limited when it comes to the deeper questions of life. They don't cope well with people's feelings, either, or with the subtleties of personal relationships or group dynamics. These all have to be 'sensed' in a different way, as we saw with the question of God. So to get a clear sense of what is happening in our lives, we Quakers try to go deeper. We have to let go our active and fretful minds in order to do this. We go quiet and let a deeper, more sensitive awareness arise. We let go of our habitual self-concern as well, because this can distort our perception of what is going on. And certainly, reasoning and debating do not of themselves help us to overcome self-interest; they can even entrench it. When we feel criticized, for example, we can quickly go on the defensive and want to justify ourselves with reasons and excuses. If on the other hand we remain still and silent, the ego quietens down, and we can *see the truth of the matter*, irrespective of how it might affect us personally. And as we open ourselves to the truth, whatever it may be, we find we are being enabled to see. We are fully attentive, but we are not actively using our minds to solve a problem. We are allowing ourselves to become fully aware of it and the situation around it, in the hope of being able to see a way through. As we do, we become aware simultaneously of a source of insight and understanding within us that is quite different from our normal, conscious self.

This is what we mean by 'Spirit'. It is not tangible or observable, and it can't be thought about directly, it's so deep and mysterious. But we know it's there because of what it does to us, and with us and through us. It enables us to see clearly what is going on – starting with what we ourselves are doing and experiencing – and it enables us to see what we can do about it, perhaps what we *have to* do. If we don't like what we see we can always reject it, deny it, but then we will lose contact with the Spirit and we won't see things clearly any more; we'll be thrown back on our own ego-based resources. We'll have to thrash it out in our minds, with the pros and cons, force ourselves to make a decision, or whatever. So we have a choice here. It is our responsibility, as I've emphasized before, what we do with the Spirit when we happen to be aware of it. If we follow its lead, we will feel its effect in our lives. We will learn to recognize it, appreciate it and, most importantly, we will learn to trust it. We will never know its reality as a matter of fact, of objective fact, as something we can prove or disprove. But we can test it in our own experience, which is partly of course subjective. Yet when it is tested in a whole group, exploring an issue together, and tested over time by the results, we can feel that the workings of the Spirit are being tested very thoroughly. And that leads to trust, to faith.

Spirit is not a supernatural force that goes against the grain of our nature. It is not irrational feeling or magical manipulation. It is our own deep nature, so that when we get in touch with it we experience it as something entirely natural. And we experience it first of all as what enlightens us. As George Fox said:

The light is that by which ye come to see.[68]
For with the light man sees himself.[69]

So spiritual awareness begins with a very down-to-earth thing: we can see what's going on, whereas previously we were deceived or hood-winked, or trying to kid ourselves, or simply fearful and prejudiced.

That is why the Spirit is so important for our regular Meetings for Business. And that is one reason why we do our business in the way we do: we want to know what's really going on so that we can do the right thing.

A second reason why we do business this way is that we recognize our limits as individuals. It is not only that we have our self-interest to think of, we also know that our experience and expertise are limited, and that other Friends have different experience, different kinds of knowledge. Variety in a group can often be seen as a disadvantage. How can people come to agree on everything if they are all so different, and from different backgrounds? Surprisingly perhaps, the Quakers see this as an advantage. Variety means we have a richer experience to draw on. It only requires that we really listen to one another, and to where we each of us come from, and we will have gained in insight from the process. If we don't do something like this, we will tend to associate with those who think as we do and disso-ciate from those who do not. We then have what Burrough called a 'controversy between party and party of men' (and of women, for that matter). We are polarized into opposite camps, because we can only see those who differ from us as opposed to us.

Much better to see everyone's experience as relevant, however limited it might be. After all, we all have some relationship to the matter we are thinking about, otherwise we wouldn't be here. And, to say the least, we can all be aware, as we wait in the Light, of the other people in the room and what is happening between us. Perhaps the women will be more aware of this than the men – that is often the gift of women. Some men may be totally absorbed in the issue to be discussed and so not be aware of the people around them – and that is their gift! So we each have something to contribute. On some matters, we have to say, one or two Friends may know a good deal more than everybody else.

They may be on the committee that has already gone through this with a tooth comb. They may be professionally trained in handling money, or bricks-and-mortar, or little children. But they need the recognition of this from the rest of the community to make their contribution helpfully and fruitfully. It is part of our job in coming to decisions that we *discern* who knows what, and what each one knows. We might say in fact that the whole process of coming to a decision is one of *discernment.* We ask ourselves, What is this really about? What are the facts of the case? Who is being affected by this, and how? Who knows what's going on, or has gone on, in cases like this? What do each of us know and/or feel about this thing? Then we can discern, finally, what is the best way forward, or what this situation requires of us.

I went through this process once in a way that impressed me deeply. It was in my old meeting in Birmingham, back in the nineties. We had just received advice from Friends House (our central body) on how to comply with the Government's new law on child protection. Anyone who is given responsibility for children in any organization must have a police check on their past record to see if they have ever been found guilty of abusing children. The advice was that we should draw up a policy to see that this was done. But it raised some of our hackles when it was presented to us in meeting. One male Friend wanted nothing to do with this interfering legislation, which implied that we trust no-one in our organization, and suspect everyone as a possible child molester. Another Friend was very nervous about the impli-cation that we *might* have such a molester in our midst, and was all in favour of implementing a tough policy. I didn't like the idea, because it seemed like we were being told what to do in our own meeting, over-riding any discernment we might have. Shouldn't we perhaps resist the State on this occasion by refusing to comply with the law? It was a heated discussion, as you can imagine, and we were not going to get a uniting Minute on this occasion. We called a Special Meeting. This time we sat in a circle without the table, and asked every one in turn – there were 10 or 12 of us – what we *felt* about the issue and what the background was in our experience that led us to feel that way. It was most enlightening. The male Friend told us of his experience as a social worker, when he had been deeply hurt by a false accusation (in court, I think it was) that blamed him for the mishandling of some children. The accusation was withdrawn, but he didn't want to have to go through such an event again, or have it dragged up in the meeting. The woman Friend admitted that she felt very nervous with children anyway and was terrified of being asked to look after them herself. Her nervousness made her feel that 'looking after children' was a dangerous and dodgy business, so she was glad to have a test run on everybody. I said I didn't like being told what to do on this matter, and, on reflection – I surprised myself saying this – I didn't like being told what to do on any matter! When we had finally gone round the circle there was a sigh of relief. We knew now where we were all coming from. We saw no reason to disagree. Instead, we found a policy that would feel right to all of us. We asked the Nominations Committee to find names for a 'children's committee' from a list of Friends who said they would be happy to work with children and happy to go through a police check for the purpose. We had a Minute to that effect, and it resolved the issue on our minds.

This then leads to the final reason why we adopt this practice. Resolving an issue this way produces great confidence in the decision and commitment to it. You can believe me when I tell you that the issue of a child protection policy didn't arise again in my old meeting. We all knew we had dealt with it properly.

We should compare this approach with what frequently happens in organizations that rely on voting or consensus. The rapid and efficient process may at first seem good. But as time goes by the people who were *out*-voted on the issue may feel at odds with the organization and resent the policy that is now in place. Those who had to compromise to achieve a consensus, which might include everybody, will feel at least slightly dissatisfied with the result, and they may harbour the wish one day to overturn it. What do the countries of Europe now feel with their new treaty for the Union? I guess they are pleased they have a treaty at all, and mildly dissatisfied that they had to surrender so much to achieve it. So what next?

Having set out these reasons for the peculiar Quaker way of doing things, we can now consider:

What is essential to the practice?

Much of the answer has already been implied in our reasons for having it. But I want to set it out in order, so that we can see the whole picture.

The first essential has to be *silence*. Once we are gathered together, with a clerk that has gone over the business we need to deal with, we sit still, in silence, to centre down. If the business meeting follows the regular Meeting for Worship, the 'centring down' will be easier, that is, we will be more able to let go of our everyday concerns and become really open, spiritually, to the matters before us. But we want to keep that openness and sensitivity throughout the meeting. It might be all too easy to get embroiled in some issue that concerns us and start leaping to our feet to get our voice heard. Or we might get bored with time being spent on 'this trivial question', and fidget or murmur to 'get on with the business'. So we need to have silence, if only a brief moment, between contributions. If the clerk feels the meeting is getting heated, or even that one Friend is, she can call for us all to be silent and centre down again.

A second factor is the need in all of us for *honesty*. This is part of what early Friends meant by 'pursuing the truth', which was not a merely intellectual affair, but a moral and practical commitment to being truthful in whatever they said or did. We can see how important this is when Friends have to weigh up our individual contribution to a meeting. They will need to know what kind of experience we are speaking from, what expertise or authority we might have on the issue in question. They will have to assess our strengths and weaknesses, so if we are not to fool them we will have to be honest with them. All this may take place subconsciously, of course, but the subtle interactions and impressions at this level can make all the difference to the outcome, and to how we live with it afterwards. Morley even recommends that we should have a moment of 'release' for any strong feelings we may have about the subject.

> Tears, harsh words, raised or shaking voices, difficulty with articulation – any of these might accompany release. Friends who release their feelings should be listened to lovingly... Sometimes we need to get something off our chests.[70]

I'm not sure about this. If feelings are aroused, or simply arise, in the course of a meeting, they should be welcomed, certainly. It may be part of the truth of our situation that we all have to face. But I'm not sure this should be expected or encouraged. Morley seems to be confusing the clarity that comes from waiting in the light with the insight that comes from allowing ourselves to feel, and to express the feeling. But expressions of strong feeling disturb the silence, and therefore confuse the clarity of the meeting. Better this, of course, than actively blocking or suppressing our feelings. When Sheeran undertook his research into American Friends during the 1970s he observed that Friends seemed to maintain their collective discipline by *not* allowing feelings to emerge.[71] To do this inevitably distorts the picture of reality we all of us get. However, from my own experience of Friends in America during the last 20 years I would say that many of them have now overcome any and every restraint they may have felt before! Is that really so much better? I asked them that once, knowing full well how restrained some of us 'Britishers' feel! What *is* better, I'm sure, is that we deal with our feelings before the meeting; and if this proves difficult because we are blocked or ashamed or fearful of feeling, we can gather a small group of Friends around us to help us deal with it. Sheeran is right, surely, when he sums up Friends' attitudes as follows:

> Friends are not opposed to emotions, not opposed to their having an important bearing on decisions. What seems important to Friends is that emotions be both deep and frankly recognized as emotions... I must know what my emotions are if I am to cope with them. So, too, must a group be aware of the feelings of its members... Although many Friends do seem to stifle their feelings, then, the mores of the meeting urge them to channel these emotions rather than to suppress them.[72]

But the point of all this is not to assess how we all individually feel about the issue, so that we can move on to how we all collectively feel about it. Feelings give us clues, markers, indications as to the reality we are facing. Once we recognize them as such we can move on to the next stage, which is to *see* the reality clearly. This then brings us to the third point, which, I hope we can now see, is central to the whole process. *The aim of the Meeting is to get beyond our individual and self-centred viewpoints to one we can all see to be valid, i.e. 'the truth', 'the best possible solution'.*
Let me quote again from Morley:

> When I am able to set my ideas aside, and you are able to set your ideas aside, doors are opened which allow solutions to enter on a shaft of Light.[73]

It needs good relations between us for this to happen, as Burrough made clear. Not in 'the way of the world', he said, not as 'party and party of men':

but in the wisdom, love and fellowship of God, in gravity, patience, meekness, in unity and concord, submitting one to another in lowliness of heart... by hearing and determining every matter coming before you in love, coolness, gentleness and dear unity.

We recognize these virtues in our everyday relationships with people, but Burrough is saying they are crucial too in the way we make decisions. It takes more than tolerance and patience to hear someone with a very different point of view. It takes a love which can encompass their different way of being in the world, and an humility in recognizing that our view is after all only our view!

But these are part negatives. There is a huge positive in this. When we are big enough really to hear one another, a space is created in which new understandings can emerge. A view might arise that no one had thought of before, and perhaps would not have been able to think of. Mixing all these different bits of life together we create the possibility of something quite *new* arising. It is a creative process, and to experience it is often quite awesome and amazing. We know then that the Spirit really is at work.

Our *Quaker Faith and Practice* urges us to take this creativity seriously and to accept the understanding that comes from it. It does so in that excellent section (3.02-3.08, see Appendix 2 here) which deals with 'the sense of the meeting':

The unity we seek depends on the willingness of us all to seek the truth in each other's utterances; on our being open to persuasion; and in the last resort on a willingness to recognize and accept the sense of the meeting as recorded in the minute, knowing that our dissenting views have been heard and considered... In a meeting rightly held a new way may be discovered which none present had alone perceived and which transcends the differences of the opinions expressed.

This is an experience of creative insight, leading to a sense of the meeting which a clerk is often led in a remarkable way to record. Those who have shared this experience will not doubt its reality and the certainty it brings of the immediate rightness of the way for the meeting to take.[74]

I will give you an example, from Barry Morley's own meeting in America. At the end of a business meeting the clerk asked if there was any other business. A woman Friend, Linda, stood up to say that she had recently walked down the lane to the meeting house... but she broke off her story to cry. Friends waited. She then, a little more composed, resumed her story. It had been Memorial Day, and she saw men with guns in the Quaker graveyard. Another Friend tried to explain:

'There are people buried in the graveyard who served in the military. The men were honoring them.'

'But they were in my graveyard with guns', Linda said through tears.

Other Friends expressed sympathy with her distress. Others expressed anger that such a thing should be allowed. But once again the situation was explained:

'They're from veterans' groups. They decorate the graves of veterans every Memorial Day'.

'After all', someone added, 'we knew they had served in the military when we allowed them to be buried there'.

This looked like stalemate. Then a Friend said:

'If a choice has to be made between Linda feeling as she does, and men with guns in the graveyard, that is not a difficult choice'.

Linda's feelings, and those of others too, had now been taken note of and recognized. An older Friend asked Linda:

'Do you have strong feelings about the veterans being remembered?'

Having been heard, and hearing the others, Linda was able to reply:

'No. I have no objection to the men being remembered.'
    'Might we allow them to decorate the graves but leave their guns outside?'

suggested the older Friend. Another Friend supported this:

'I can approve of that if it is acceptable to Linda'.
'Yes,' said Linda, 'I would find that acceptable'.
The meeting fell silent, and then adjourned.

A year later, quite unexpectedly, Linda reported to the meeting that she had visited the graveyard on Memorial Day to check on the veterans.
    'They left their guns outside when they went in', she said.
    'The silence that followed', comments Morley, 'amplified the sense of unity we had felt a year earlier'.[75]
    That is a good example of creative resolution. We may wonder why Friends did not seem to pick up on the moral rightness of what Linda was saying, and focused on her feeling, but that is how the dilemma was presented to them, and they found a way through it. Perhaps the most important move was that they were able to understand and sympathize with Linda's strong feeling, even if they didn't all share it, so they created a bond of unity. And when the creative solution was proposed – you can see that it was more than a compromise – Friends were able, as they say,

'to unite on it'. And that unity, as Morley recognizes, gave them the assurance that they were making the right decision.

That, as it happens, indicates the final point I want to make about what is essential to the practice. *We know we have the right decision when we have unity,* having avoided (or overcome) polarization and conflict. It is the skill of the clerk in a meeting to recognize, not only the sense of the meeting, but the unity that it brings. She may discover this by 'trying out a Minute', to see what objections or reservations there may be to it. She is also, in this testing, trying out the form of words that would best express this understanding. When the final Minute is written and accepted by the meeting, it then has authority in the meeting. It is not simply a record of 'what we have decided', which we might conceivably change if we change our minds. It is a record of how we, together, have been led to act by the Spirit within us.

What makes all this possible?

We can see that this is as much a spiritual exercise as our Meeting for Worship. Although we do not come together specifically to 'worship' on this occasion – we come to do business – we do come in the same attitude of openness and receptivity, and we expect in the same way to be guided by the Spirit. (That shows we can be as spiritual in deciding an action as we are in contemplation. In fact it is part of our Quaker way to carry the insights we gain in worship into the life of action, into the everyday.) But for all this we have to take some responsibility to see that this happens. We have to put ourselves in a position where we *can* be open and receptive, both to the issues themselves and to the Spirit working quietly within us. So over the years Friends have developed a certain pattern of behaviour which can facilitate the process. You will see much of this recorded in *Quaker Faith and Practice* (chapter 3 mostly, as in Appendix 2 here, but it pervades the whole book). It will help, though, if I pull it together so that we can see it as a whole. What makes the Quaker way of deciding an issue practicable, then, is that:

We pause between contributions,
> not jumping in as soon as we get a chance, and not interrupting.

We speak to the meeting as a whole,
> not to an individual in particular, especially not to the Friend who has just spoken.

We defer to the clerk.
> Like the players in an orchestra, we wait till we have a cue from the 'conductor' that we are free to speak. In a large meeting this normally involves standing up or raising a hand and waiting to be called. In a small meeting a look or a nod may be enough.
>
> These three could be summed up by the advice of George Fox, 'Be still and cool in thy own mind and spirit from thy own thoughts'.[76]

We listen attentively to everyone,
> even the least articulate or knowledgeable.

We speak briefly and to the point,
> avoiding the desire to make a speech.

We avoid rhetoric and manipulation,
> which may persuade people temporarily, but not convince them deeply.

We may prepare our minds beforehand, but not our opinions!
> The clerk has to bear that in mind too, since anxiety about an item on the agenda may persuade her to settle her own mind about it first.
>
> These four can be summed up by Fox's words again: 'Let truth be the head, and practise it'.[77]

We keep silent while the clerk writes a Minute.
> The temptation is to chatter while the clerk scribbles quietly at the table, but she is trying to get 'the sense of the meeting', so she needs our quiet support.

We unite on a Minute, not on a vote.

> We're looking to agree, not on the proposal that carries the day, but the form of words which expresses the sense of the whole meeting.

We delay till another meeting if unity is not achievable.

> Even if only one member cannot accept the Minute, it will be better for the meeting, and the decision, if we wait until we can all accept it – whatever it then is.

We submit to the Minute once it is accepted,

> which is a test of how seriously we take the process of being led by the Spirit.
>
> These last four may be summed up briefly by Fox's 'Mind the oneness'.

These are not rules, in the strict sense. They are models of good practice. There are no sanctions against not following them, but our experience has been, historically, that if we do not follow the practice we shall miss out on the clarity and confidence that come with it. But Friends find that out for themselves. It is part of the experimental nature of our faith that we test our practice continually by experience, if only to confirm, sometimes, that we got it right the first time. Once we are (re)assured of this, we can commit ourselves wholeheartedly to the discipline, and hold on in faith when the process seems to be stuck or dragging on endlessly. Nothing is more heartening than to see it come right in the end.

What makes it difficult?

This needs to be added as a postscript really, because we have to admit in honesty that the process of communal enlightenment does sometimes seem to be impossible. This is most obviously the case when one or other of the above conditions cannot be met. For example, Friends *are* sometimes attached to their opinions and might find it particularly hard to let go if their favoured opinion is being attacked in meeting. Their usually wide experience of doing business in the secular world inevitably establishes a habit of mind that is difficult to break in a gathering of Friends. Both these facts show how important it is to be silent before the discussion begins. My own experience of serving on the union committee of my university taught me a thing or two about how to get my own way: form a caucus of like-minded people beforehand and plan a strategy; make over-strong demands so that the inevitable compromise turns out to be exactly what you want; lobby the influential members beforehand to 'share your concern'; get agreement on overall aims and strategies so that you can use them later to exclude what others might want to do. I also learnt from this, much later, that this was also a good way of not making friends, and not making good decisions!

There is an individual equivalent to this bad committee practice. I can suppress voices in myself if I want a strong desire or fear in me to be met. This is a quite normal way of dealing with inner conflicts, as we shall see later, but it can also play mischievously in meetings and committees as well as in ourselves. Instead of dealing with the issues truthfully and honestly in a meeting, we dull our sensitivity and project our dark thoughts or desires onto the situation we are discussing, badly misrepresenting it. This is something which also takes discipline and watchfulness to deal with.

At the other end of the scale, a very large meeting of Friends presents its own difficulties. A Yearly Meeting in session can have as many as one thousand Friends present. How then do we 'hear every voice' that needs to be heard? How do we get to know them well enough to 'know where they're coming from' and learn to cope with the differences? Above all, how does the Yearly Meeting clerk discern 'the sense of the meeting'? It does happen, I know, but how? I have no real answers to these questions, but I hope this discussion will stimulate you to think about them.

Chapter five

Living Faithfully

We have now seen how we deal with the problems we face as a group. We have a well established method for doing that. With matters for personal decision, however, we are less well assured. We have lost the discipline we once had, many years ago. So part of what I want to do here is to remind you of that discipline, and suggest how it might be applied in our new, modern situation.

But let me remind you, first of all, of what we have discussed so far about the Quaker approach to spirituality. You should then see how our present theme follows on inevitably, and naturally.

I was saying that in our spiritual quest we Quakers rely first of all on the resources we each have within us. We turn to other people for help, obviously, and we read books or papers to gain knowledge and insight. But first of all we rely on ourselves, or rather, on the deep resource within us we call 'the light' and 'the spirit'. We therefore have no priests or ordained ministers, no official teaching or creed, and no sacred books that we regard as finally authoritative, all of which presuppose that the truth or strength we need in life is outside us. In this respect we are unlike every other Christian group, and unlike most other religious groups around the world. Some people think we are foolish to deny ourselves the benefit of these external supports. Still others wonder how we can still call ourselves Christian or religious when we have none of the marks that distinguish a religion. But foolish or not, Christian or not, this is the fact about Quakers we most need to understand.

The Quaker way of living

This then provides the background for understanding how Quakers live their lives. *They live their lives, their practical, everyday lives, as they are led by the Spirit within them.* That, I think, is a sound general statement about the Quaker way, but it needs to be amplified a bit to avoid some misunderstandings. It does not mean, for example, that Quakers live just as they wish to, as they are led by the whim or desire of the moment. The 'Spirit' that leads has nothing to do with the whim of the moment; it is not itself a feeling or an emotion. It is deep down within us, and manifests itself only as we let go the claims of the ego, including our selfish desire, and let its voice be heard, or its light shine. The voice within 'speaks to our condition', and the light shows us the truth of our life, so when we say we are 'led by the Spirit', we mean that we live in response to the reality of our life as the Spirit shows it to us. This can often be quite challenging, because we might not want to face the reality of our life or do the kind of thing it seems to require. Our desire may conflict with what the Spirit requires.

On the other hand, 'being led by the Spirit' does not mean following a strict code of ethics, not even the code of 'Quaker values'. Unfortunately, Friends have taken a liking to 'values' in recent years, because they don't know how else to describe the basic Quaker commitment. Our life then is supposedly based on a set of 'beliefs and values', described perhaps in our *Book of Discipline*, which we try to put into practice. A recent publication from our Yearly Meeting described our historic 'testimonies' as bearing witness to our basic 'beliefs and values', though it could not then proceed to tells us what those values were. This is understandable if we recognize that that is how other people are likely to see us and describe us; all religious and philosophical groups are supposedly based on a set of beliefs and values, that is, things which could be written down on paper as representing what is true and good. But having put it like that, we can see that that *couldn't* be what Quakers do, not really. They accept as their basic truth what is not and cannot be written on a piece of paper. And it is a truth that each of them has to see for themselves. In fact, knowing how to live is precisely a matter of seeing for oneself and responding to the truth of what one sees with an open heart.

This sounds risky, I have to admit. A lot of people will object that living without rules or 'standards' is irresponsible and dangerous, and could lead to anarchy. They objected to the first Quakers for exactly this reason. They deserve a reply. Three things, I think, can be said:

1. As we have seen, the Quaker experience is that, when we open ourselves to the truth of our life, our self-deceptions and denials are revealed, including the false image we have of ourselves, and at the same time we discover the true self that lies behind these images. We discover who we really are, not isolated and apart from others, but one with them, and with life itself. This awareness awakens a great feeling for life, and for others, that we can only call love. As we hold on to that truth we find love growing within us, until it overcomes the feelings of fear and anxiety that might have motivated us before. We are able to act out of love, that is, out of warm respect for other people and other creatures, so that we want spontaneously to help them and not harm them. Now with that feeling, we do not need laws and commandments to tell us what to do. 'Love is the fulfilment of the law', as Paul the Apostle said, so we don't have to try to fulfil the law, which we will never do anyway, not completely and wholeheartedly (see Romans 13, 1 Corinthians 13). 'The quality of mercy is not strained', said Shakespeare. Love and mercy are spontaneous responses of the heart to a world in pain, a world in God. What holds us back is not a lack of effort or education, but fear and the false sense of self. Let the light remove these, and we are free to love, free to live from our own true self. We don't even need 'Quaker values'!

2. We can prepare the way for this opening of the heart and we

can guard against the temptation to close it again. We will of course feel antagonistic towards people from time to time, because people can be annoying and we can feel insecure and resentful. These things will happen.We can't expect to be free of them. When the early Friends said they could be 'perfect' they didn't have in mind what we mean by the term, free from all fault and blemish, perfect in every respect. They meant they had the power to act rightly and to resist the temptation to put self first. But they had to exercise that power. They had to be watchful, and when they fell down they had to pick themselves up again. None of it could be taken for granted. But if they put their mind to it, they found, they could live as they really wanted to live. And we could have that confidence too, if we continue to let the light show us the truth. That commitment to truth is our core discipline, and it's that that ensures that the love will flow. Similarly, the experience of love, and of being loved, encourages us to stay with the truth. As Gandhi said (no Quaker, certainly, but a man very sympathetic to Quakers): 'Love and truth are two sides of the same coin'[78].

3. We can also commit ourselves to the path of truth and love even when we don't feel like it. That may seem to contradict what I said earlier about relying on the feeling for others that arises when we open ourselves to the way things are. But we have to recognize that our deeper feelings can be clouded over by the anxieties of the moment, by tiredness or disappointment. We then have to trust that the deeper feeling is still there, buried somewhere, and act on that trust. Also, we don't always understand very well the situation we are in, and may have to wait a while until it gets clearer. But our experience is that when we act on the understanding we do have, and wait in the light for further enlightenment, it does become clearer. So there is a pattern and a process to living a faithful life, and that ensures that, if we follow it, we will do the right thing.

These misunderstandings of Quaker practice show us that we people of the modern world find it difficult to grasp what the Quaker thing is really about. We understand the world out there very well, and we analyse it and talk about it endlessly. But we don't generally understand the inner life, the illumination of our life by the Spirit, or the value of silent waiting, without words. These things have to be learned, against the grain of our modern way of doing things, and we Quakers have to start learning them and teaching them.

The role of advice

A good model for thinking about our practical life is provided by that introductory section of *Quaker Faith and Practice* called 'Advices and Queries'. This is very practical and down-to-earth advice about how we might conduct ourselves in the modern world, from family and sex life, to business and politics. But at no point does it lay down the law about what we *ought* to do. (I may be wrong, but I don't think the words 'ought' and 'must' ever appear in the text.) It is never more that the title suggests, *Advices and Queries*. It has even been suggested, though I can't confirm this, that the Quakers invented the query as a form of religious discourse, and that they did this at the very beginning of the movement. We have been sending one another 'queries' ever since, challenging one another to consider and reconsider what we're doing with our lives. One of the first queries we sent out, to all the meetings around the country, is still worth our putting to ourselves: How does truth prosper among you? The Yearly Meeting was not asking about doctrines or official teaching, of course; 'truth' meant the reality that Friends had discovered for themselves as they opened their hearts to the truth of their own life. The question was, or the query was, whether that sense of reality was still alive, and whether Friends still lived in it and bore witness to it with their lives.

During the first big crisis of the movement, in 1656, the elders of Balby Meeting in Yorkshire decided they had to establish some discipline among Friends – James Nayler, hero though he was, had set a bad example to Friends, and given the wrong message to the rest of the world, when he rode into Bristol on the back of a donkey. He had imitated Christ with good intentions, no doubt: as a testimony to the fact, denied by the official teaching, that everyone had Christ within them, whether they knew it or not. It was taken, however, as an act of blasphemy and seized upon by the authorities as a pretext for stamping out the movement. To stop that happening, Friends had to take action, and the elders of Balby realized that it required at least that Friends learn to discipline themselves and not act on 'leadings' impulsively. But in the Epistle they drafted they came near to laying down the law on what Friends could do and not do. They must have realized this themselves, because they then immediately added a postscript that has come to be a treasure for Friends ever since – it has been repeated, I believe, in every Book of Discipline published after that. It is now at the end of 1.01 (see Appendix 3), which concludes the introduction to *Advices and Queries:*

> Dearly beloved Friends, these things we do not lay upon you as a rule or form to walk by, but that all, with the measure of light that is pure and holy, may be guided; and so in the light walking and abiding, these may be fulfilled in the Spirit, not from the letter, for the letter killeth, but the Spirit giveth life.

The first part is perhaps well known: these advices are not to be taken as fixed rules that Friends have to comply with. The second part is less well known, or at least, less well understood: the reason for their saying this is not that Friends must make up their own minds, or that the elders of Balby were uncertain about the advice they were giving, but because they knew that whatever wisdom they had obtained on this difficult matter had come from the Spirit within them, and since the Spirit was also in the Friends they were writing to, Friends should consult *that* in order to get a proper understanding and appreciation of what the elders were saying. In fact the elders' Epistle was intended only to help Friends 'be guided' by the Spirit. But notice their reference to 'the measure of light that is pure and holy', which we have come across before. The elders were aware that not all Friends had the same 'measure' of understanding in these things and that some Friends could do with help. That, in a nutshell, is the unique Quaker way of supporting one another while not dominating or manipulating one another.

How does it work in practice?

We asked this question in relation to the Quaker business method, and some of the answers apply to our decisions in everyday life. In fact, the business method exemplifies all our decision-making very well. It is a method for our deciding things together, so we all have to be aware of it and practise it consciously. It would be good then to ask ourselves, when we have a difficult decision before us, how would we go about dealing with this in a Meeting for Business?

Thomas Kelly gives a good example of how to do this in his searching little book on spirituality, *A Testament of Devotion:*[79]

> We Western peoples are apt to think our great problems are external, environmental. We are not skilled in the inner life, where the real roots of our problem lie... The outer distractions of our interests reflect an inner lack of integration of our own lives. We are trying to be several selves at once, without all our selves being organized by a single, mastering Life within us. Each of us tends to be, not a single self, but a whole committee of selves.[80]

Kelly then develops this idea that we are each like a committee:

It is as if we have a chairman of our committee of the many selves within us, who does not integrate the many into one but who merely counts the votes at each decision, and leaves disgruntled minorities...

If the Society of Friends has anything to say, it lies in this region primarily. Life is meant to be lived from a Centre, a divine Centre.[81]

He cites as a model for us the American Friend, John Woolman, who made his name in the world by his opposition to slavery and by the simplification of his life that freed him from dependence on the work of slaves:

His outward life became simplified... He didn't have to struggle, and renounce, and strain to achieve simplicity. He yielded to the Centre and his life became simple... His many selves were integrated into a single true self, whose whole aim was humbly walking in the presence and guidance and will of God. There was no shouting down of a disgruntled minority by a majority vote among his selves. It was as if there were in him a presiding chairman who, in the solemn, holy silence of inwardness, took the sense of the meeting. I would suggest that the Quaker method of conducting business meetings is also applicable to the conduct of our individual lives, inwardly.[82]

So how might we do that? Reflecting on what was said last time about the business method, some obvious answers come to mind. They suggest to me a process of decision-making, tailored to our personal needs.

1. The first thing is to *become still and silent*, to allow the natural concerns of the ego to quieten down. So we obviously have to find a time and a place when we can do that, without the fear of

interruption. Some of us might be able to do that by going for a walk or taking a bath. The important thing is to be able to relax mentally and to be attentive to whatever might come up from within.

2. We could then *identify the issue* that concerns us. It may not be immediately obvious, after all, and the matter that does weigh on our minds may not be the real issue. As early Friends said, we have to 'look to the light in our consciences', that is, to become aware of whatever it is our conscience is troubled about, which may not be easy for us if we suspect that we might have some responsibility here! But this is what our first Advice advises us to do, and it gives us two good reasons for taking this difficult path: 'Take heed, dear Friends to the promptings of love and truth in your hearts. Trust them as the leadings of God whose Light shows us our darkness and brings us to new life.' (See Appendix 3, from *Quaker Faith and Practice* 1.02.) These faint promptings, these nudges of the conscience, are to be taken seriously because they are 'leadings' from God and, if followed, will shed light on our lives, dispelling the confusion and pretence, and give us new life. That of course is a recommendation for our whole life, but it can apply too in the specifics of life, whenever we face difficulty or choice.

3. In this attitude of waiting and expectancy, aware of the issue that really concerns us deep down, we can then give our attention to what is really going on there. As in a meeting for business, we can try to put our self-interest aside and *look for the truth*. That is where the discipline comes in, because we will certainly be tempted to explain the situation in a way that lets us off the hook completely, or conversely, that assures us that we are the ones to blame - as usual! The thing is to see things as they are, without blaming or excusing anybody. When we get a sense of the unvarnished truth we will be in a position to act; we will know what

needs to be done. But because these insights arise as we wait in the light, without our trying to resolve the issue ourselves, they will be experienced as 'coming' to us. We are 'being shown' the truth. We are 'being led' to do the right thing.

4. Before we then act on this, however, we have to reflect on what we are being shown. Ask ourselves, if this is true what I'm seeing, what are the implications? Where do I need to change my thinking, or my whole feeling about this thing? What we come to see in the silence may in fact be very close to what we thought before, but it may not. It may be very new and surprising, and it will need some adjusting to. However long it takes, though, we have to *accept the implications* of the insights we get.

5. Only then can we, finally, *take action*. Perhaps we have only enough insight to take the first step. We must be careful then not to jump ahead of the game, 'not to run ahead of our guide', as early Friends put it. Yet taking action after a process of reflection like that will seem very right and very firm. There will be no 'disgruntled minorities', as Kelly called them, but a feeling of rightness, even of peace. Like the experience of unity in a meeting, when the sense of the meeting has been followed, we will have the good feeling that confirms that we have indeed done the right thing.

I hope that process makes sense. If it doesn't immediately make sense it would be good to try it out quite consciously and deliberately as an exercise. Our Quaker processes, after all, are open to experiment and testing. However, the real benefit of this practice can be felt only when we do it regularly over a period of time. A daily practice is probably the best. From the beginning Friends have committed themselves to a daily exercise of 'retirement' or meditation, though there are many ways of doing this. One kind of practice is described by Donald Court:

I could not face the next day without a time in which life is renewed. I shall not describe this in detail. The essence is regularity and time – time to reach down to the level where I can begin to see myself and my work straight, where that strength we call love can break through my anxiety and teach me how to respond instead of react, where I am not ruled by conscience but by Jesus the true man within; the level where I can accept my whole nature and forgive myself and others... Prayer alone can reopen the road to the spirit, blocked repeatedly by busy-ness, self-importance, self-indulgence, self-pity, depression or despair.[83]

More recently, some of us have been experimenting with the earliest Quaker practice. It arose from my own study of the early Quakers, when they advised one another on how to access the light and find the truth that would transform their lives. We follow their practice, with a modern twist, by:

1. relaxing for a few minutes, to become receptive and attentive,
2. looking to see what issues arise that need our attention,
3. focusing on one issue that presents itself, to see the whole reality of it,
4. asking why it is like that, but waiting for the answer to come,
5. welcoming the answer, when it comes, accepting the implications, and
6. finally, checking how we now feel about it, deep down, and what action we need to take.

I've written about this elsewhere, if you want to follow it up.[84] It's worth trying out, especially in a group of Friends, where you can share your experiences afterwards. But the point is, we need *some* practice that we can undertake regularly and comfortably.

The Quaker way takes us further than this, however. It expects us to put our given insights into action, to *live* what we come to see in the light. This way we can test our insights over time, to see if they match reality as lived, and if they are valid we will gain more insight in the process. There is an interesting account of the life of Mary Hughes that tells us something of what 'living in the light' might mean. She spent much of her life, nearly 100 years ago, living and working among the poor in London.

> She didn't want to *visit* the poor. She wanted to be *with* the poor and to be poor herself... She had no set schemes. She founded no institutions... She became a magnet [that]... drew the poor and dispossessed, there was plenty to do; and Mary Hughes went about the doing of it in her own idiosyncratic way... She never turned down man or woman who had duped or bamboozled her. It was in the nature of things that the world contained sinners, and she wished above all to live close to the nature of things. This she could confidently do because of her belief that the overriding reality is spiritual.[85]

The test of her unusual leading is that she was able really to help the poor. And she was able to be effective partly because she kept her nose to the ground and was truly open to the people she met. In the sense that early Friends gave to it, she was 'a friend of the truth'. I like that phrase, 'to live close to the nature of things'. It echoes the phrase of Donald Court I quoted before, 'to see myself and my work straight'. The one follows from the other. The one enriches the other. When we 'see our work straight', for example, we will know better what to do in our work and how to do it. Then putting our insights into action we will be able to 'live close to the nature of things', working effectively, learning more as we go, and we will also be able to test our insights in the experience.

The other way of testing our insights, or the 'leading' as to what we should do, is to share it with other Friends. If we are entangled in something, others' objectivity might help us through. If we are one-sided, their different viewpoints will balance us up. If we only get part of the picture, they may help to see the whole. The best example of this is another practice of early Friends that has been recently revived, 'the clearness committee'.[86] When a Friend faces a difficult decision, or a big one like getting married (or divorced), going for a job or taking retirement, he or she can call a 'clearness committee'. She can ask a couple of close Friends that she knows will understand, an overseer and elder maybe, and perhaps a Friend from another meeting with some experience or expertise in this area. They then meet for an hour or two, with silences between their contributions, while she explains her dilemma or situation as fully as she needs to and Friends listen attentively, without interruption. They then ask her questions that should enable her see her situation more clearly, to get a wider perspective or an alternative view. They do not give her advice or 'answers'. Out of this experience the 'discernment' of what to do should grow, perhaps over the next few days or weeks. I attended a clearness committee for a Friend of mine, Dick, who was wondering whether to accept the offer of a place in a Quaker retirement home. He put his dilemma to us. He may not get another offer for some time, and he did need support now that he was getting too frail to go shopping and make his own meals. He was a bit lonely too, his wife having died a year or two previously. On the other hand, the house still had a lot of meaning for him, and it helped him to mourn his loss by living there. Though he was now more limited in what he could do, he valued the fact that he had some control of his life. After a period of silence we began to ask him questions: What support did he really need? Was he clinging to past memories? What was so attractive about living in the house? It was the last question which really stayed with Dick, as he pondered it in the next few days. He wrote to us all to tell us that he had come to realize that the most important thing for him at present was his independence. So he had written to the retirement home to tell them that he would not accept the offer at this time. (He arranged for Social Services to do his shopping and cook his meals – in his house – which resolved another issue rather well.) As it happens, he got a second offer of a room a year later and, feeling differently about the situation, he accepted it. He moved to the home with the strong confidence that it was the right thing to do, and this in turn helped him to cope with the emotional upheaval that the move brought with it.

Living against the grain

Simple and natural it may be, but 'living faithfully' is not easy in the modern world, because it is going against the grain. The modern way of living is, for the most part, very different. It gives a lot of emphasis to the needs and choices of the individual. Whatever the individual really wants is what the individual ought to get. So much of our social and political life is built around the 'supply' of what people 'demand'. The people vote for the party that can give them most of what they have decided they want. Similarly, business and trade revolves, not around needs, real needs, but wants, much of which business and trade have stimulated and directed through advertising. Personal morality is much influenced by all this, so that people make choices in order to meet desires. It goes something like this: if you want to know the right thing to do in your life or with your life, you have to:

1. Look to your own interest first of all, making sure you understand your main interest and your long-term interest,
2. acknowledge your debt to society, which enabled you to become what you are, which means you should at least abide by its rules, which are designed to meet the interests

of society as a whole (or at least a significant or powerful part of it),

3. acknowledge your debt to God, if you believe in God (in the traditional sense), because this all-powerful being should be able to reconcile the interests of 1 and 2, perhaps by rewarding you in a life after death for your faithful compliance with the rules of society.

Notice that the modern way is very reasonable and realistic – unfettered by what moderns may see as the idealism of people like Quakers - but that it is also riddled with conflict. 'I' am pitted against 'society' and both against 'God' (if God is brought into the equation at all). There are also then the conflicts within myself, since every desire has a claim, the conflicts with the other individuals with whom I share my life, and conflicts between my 'society', the group I identify with, and other 'societies'. The modern way of life, for all its great advances, is made up of egos and the groups they form to sustain and protect themselves. For this reason too, the modern way of life tends to separate individuals from one another, even to isolate them, which encourages them further to look to their own (individual) interest, and to support their increasingly fragile sense of identity by accumulating 'things'. This is to over-simplify, I know, but I describe it thus briefly just to highlight the contrast, and to show how the Quaker way has to go against the grain to be faithful to its insights, while at the same time pointing society to another, less destructive way.

But I want to conclude by emphasising that 'living faithfully' does not mean living naively or idealistically, as is sometimes suggested. Our response to the mainstream is not to brandish ideals and values that we urge others to follow, but, surprisingly perhaps, to get to the truth we have all been ignoring, and to point to the truth in every way we can. (That 'pointing' will be our theme in the next chapter.) Our sense is that the modern way of life, for all its supposed realism, is based on an illusion about who we humans are, and this is the main reason for all the conflicts and suffering we experience in the world. Our first move then is to discover who we really are, beyond the conscious egos that claim our attention, and to discover that we are indeed more than the separate individuals we appear to be, because we are bound together by life. In our meditations together and alone, we dive under the water, so to speak, and discover that the separate islands we inhabit are not really separate at all, but united under the sea. This new awareness of ourselves is the basis for a new understanding of what humans can be like. As we try to live out that understanding we discover indeed that this is a new and better way of being human. We experience a new validity and authenticity in our life, and we experience a harmony with each other which greatly enriches us. Beyond selfish desires and manufactured wants, we discover real love, and find that we in turn are able to give love.

I leave you with a letter from the early Quaker writer Elizabeth Bathurst, urging Friends, initially, to love one another as they have been taught by God inwardly to do so:

For we are taught of God to love one another (1 Thess 4.9), and by this shall all men know that we are the disciples of Christ (John 13.35). Thus as they behold our comely order, while we live in love together, like children of one father, and in the inward union dwell, so shall they discern the splendour of the truth to shine in and amongst us, even like an orient pearl. And so shall we be bound up together in the bundle of love and life in Christ Jesus, and shall grow up in him like willows by the water courses and as tender plants which God's right hand hath planted.[87]

Chapter six

Bearing Witness

How do we communicate to others what is most important for us as Quakers? Do we have a message? And if so, how do we get it across? These are difficult questions for Quakers, it has to be said, but it will surely do us some good if we face them. One difficulty is that we do not have the kind of answer to life's problems that could be spelt out in a philosophy or doctrine that we could then teach to others. We have no 'gospel' as other churches understand the term, and we have no official doctrine which we can explain when people ask us, as inevitably they do, what do Quakers believe? We are very concerned not to be seen as 'having all the answers'. In an important sense we are still all 'seekers', and always will be. So to talk openly and publicly about what we are committed to, and why, could seem arrogant. We don't want in any sense to proselytize. So we are in fact very reticent about our faith, and rather invisible to the world out there.

Behind this reticence and reserve, however, there is an assumption that if we have something to 'bear witness to' it has to be a fundamental belief, and that since Quakers today have many different beliefs there is really not that much we can say for ourselves, as a body of Quakers. Perhaps just that 'there is that of God in everyone'. (Ben Pink Dandelion's sociological research has shown that that is indeed the only belief that modern, liberal Friends have in common[88].) Some recent outreach booklets have solved this problem by asking twelve Quakers to write what they individually believe, and they leave it at that.

But this assumption shows a serious misunderstanding of Quaker truth, as we have discussed this in the last few chapters. The truth that really helps us, we have found, is not the kind that can easily be put in words, and it is therefore not easily formulated as a belief. It is, first of all, the truth of our own life. We have to look at it and accept it for ourselves. This is not easy, we know, because we are all wary of truth, in this direct, personal sense, and the temptation is to deny it, and therefore to pretend that our life is other than it really is. But if we do accept it, we find that the truth is liberating, and gives us a sense of our own true selves, free from all the pretence. We are able to live more freely and fully as we mostly deeply wish to. We also become aware of the larger reality in which our life is set, the reality of our family and social life, the global reality of our world, and finally, the ultimate reality which is the basis of everything, including our own life. If we sense that reality and live in response to it, we feel we belong and we sense a deep kinship with other human beings and with other creatures. Indeed, we *feel* for others more, finding their own unhappiness or trouble weighing on us, and we will understand better why they are in that situation. We then recognize that others need the kind of understanding and awareness we have found by waiting in the light.

That is a summary, if you like, of what we Quakers have found over the centuries. We don't know it always that clearly or fully, but we do know it; it is that that draws us on in the Quaker life and inspires us to live more fully in this way. In particular – and this is the main point of my describing this experience - it leads to two impulses which are central to Quaker life, and which have shaped our history.

Two desires

There is first the desire to *bear witness to the truth* we have discerned, so that others will recognize it too, and be liberated by it. And there is also the desire to *overcome the evils of the world* that cause such misery and suffering. These desires are clearly linked – perhaps at bottom they are different aspects of the same desire – but it will be helpful initially to distinguish them. The desire to share our truth follows directly from the experience we were discussing last time, in the context of our personal life, so we will deal with this first. The desire to change the world will be our theme in the next chapter.

So *why* we bear witness is not (if we are well grounded as Quakers) to impose our truth on the world, ignoring how others see it or experience it, but to share our discovery so that they can discover it too, in their life and in their way. And *what* we bear witness to is a truth which we discern is somehow true for everyone. That universal dimension has to be 'discerned' by distinguishing what is peculiar to me and to us – our truth – from what is applicable to everyone. We can do that when we go deeply enough into our own experience to sense what is basically human, and when we share our experience with others to find what we have in common. But part of our discovery is that we humans are alike, we are of 'one blood', 'one mould', as Fox liked to put it. Differences between people are often used to obscure this; they can become part of an illusion, which we can learn to break through. So we can be brave in our witnessing because it can really do some good in helping people to come to themselves.

But how?

Communicating truth

We communicate our truth, we say, by 'bearing witness'. That is our established Quaker phrase. Like the word 'testimony', 'witness' is a key word in our history, as much now as at the beginning. And the *way* we bear witness tells us as much about the Quaker movement as what we bear witness to. But what do we mean by these words?

The phrase 'bearing witness' comes originally from the law court. Every use of the phrase outside of the law court is now something of a metaphor. When someone is accused of a crime 'witnesses' are called to the stand so that they can give us a first-hand account of what they saw and heard that is relevant to the situation, or give an expert account of what generally happens in these cases on the basis of their specialized knowledge. What the witness says has authority because he or she knows from experience what happened (or what generally happens), and others in the court do not, including the judge and the lawyers. The witnesses will not be able to *prove* that what they say is true – the evidence is not available for everyone to see. In that respect a law court is very different from a scientific laboratory, though both are trying to establish the truth on the basis of the evidence before them. Scientific evidence is repeatable, at least in principle, and if not, it cannot count as evidence. Legal evidence is not repeatable, or not often; it is unique, one-off. 'This is what happened at 7 o'clock in the evening in the market place in Lancaster. I was there, I saw it all happen.' That is the language of the witness, or as we say, that is his or her 'testimony'. We generally have to trust the witness, otherwise we lose the truth we need as a society to survive. (Because of the vital importance of the testimony and our general suspicion that the witness may not tell the truth, the state has invented the dubious ritual of making a witness swear solemnly on the Bible that they will 'tell the truth, the whole truth, and nothing but the truth.')

I've laboured all this because it will help us to understand why Quakers do the things they do, which is in so many way different from what others do.

Quaker faith and life, as we have seen, are based on experience, not on official teaching. We have discovered a truth, certainly, and it makes a difference to our lives, but it is not something we can 'show' to other people. It is not out there in the public sphere as 'evidence' that people can investigate and consider. In this respect it is slightly different from what a legal witness may 'witness'. Perhaps only *he* saw what happened, but if someone else had been there, they would have seen it as well. The jury in a court at least has to recognize the experience the witness is describing as the kind of experience they might have had. So what can we do? We can only hope, as we bear witness, that others will recognize what we say or do from their own experience. We are in that respect in the same position as John in the New Testament who wrote in his first epistle:

> It was there from the beginning; we have heard it; we have seen it with our own eyes; we looked upon it, and felt it with our own hands; our theme is the Word which gives life. This life was made visible; we have seen it and bear our testimony; we declare to you the eternal life which was with the Father and was made visible to us. It is this which we have seen and heard that we declare to you also, in order that you may share with us a common life[89]

What John had to say in his epistle (and his more famous Gospel) was well-grounded from his point of view, but what if his readers didn't recognize the experience on which it was based? That is precisely our dilemma. What do most people imagine we can experience by waiting in stillness and silence? Even George Fox was aware of this problem. Writing to some confident intellectuals of his time, he said:

> All you that be in your own wisdom and in your own reason, you tell that silent waiting upon God is famine to you; it is a strange life to you to come to be silent, you must come into a new world. Now you must die in the silence, die from the wisdom... and die from the understanding.[90]

That's quite a lot to ask, to give up their intellectualizing entirely. And why should they do that if they cannot grasp the experience that would be gained from it?

Is this a cul-de-sac for Friends?

Not quite. It's the end of one road, we might say, but it's also a challenge to find another road, another way through. In our explorations over the years we have found three other ways of communicating:

1. We may speak to something deeper in people than their conscious thoughts. What they consciously think about themselves and the world may not encompass all that they know or experience. Indeed, what they think in their heads may run counter to what they know in their hearts; that deeper knowledge may be too obscure for them to recognize, or too uncomfortable to face. Their ideas might then be intended (unconsciously perhaps) to silence or smother the deeper thoughts within them. And it is that deeper awareness in people that Quakers are trying to address. They are trying to 'answer that of God' in people. They cannot (successfully) argue for this deeper truth, since argument will only engage the conscious mind and perhaps provoke a defensive reaction. They have to be more personal in their form of address, perhaps challenging people to think and feel in a new way. How they do this precisely will have to be determined by the situation they are in, their relationship with the people they want to touch. They will have to *sense* what is required. They will want to speak the truth of course, but only 'in love', as the Apostle Paul says[91]. This may require them to speak indirectly, using images, poetic phrases, or stories to convey their meaning. The story of their own experience may be the best they can tell, since it invites the hearers to recognize parallels in their own life. This autobiographical style has been a predominant form of communication for Friends since the very beginning of their movement. Fox wrote his *Journal,* virtually inventing the autobiography as a way of conveying spiritual truth,[92] and he has been followed by many Friends since. The point of such stories, however, is to evoke an awareness in others of their own true story, that is, to evoke a knowledge they already have of themselves which they might be denying or simply unable to discern. This is what Fox meant by

'answering that of God' in people. It was not answering in our sense, replying to a question, but, in an older use of the word, matching or echoing what was already going on for them. And Friends generally have the confidence that what is going on for people, deep down (whatever they may say or do), is that something of God is nudging and prodding them to accept the truth and live it.

2. There is something else Friends can do. They can invite people to try the Quaker method for themselves. They are not, after all, expecting people to believe what they say 'on trust'. They are hoping they will try it for themselves and discover from their own experience the validity of the Quaker witness. William Penn made this point in the Preface to his impressive, early account of the Quaker movement:[93]

> Not that thou shouldst believe upon my authority, nothing less – for that's not to act upon knowledge, but trust – but that thou shouldst try and approve [test and verify] what I write, for that is all I ask, as well as all I need, for thy conviction [for you to be convinced] and my own justification [and for me to be proved right]. The whole, indeed, being but a spiritual experiment upon the soul, and therefore seeks for no implicit credit, because it is self-evident to them that will uprightly try it [put it to the test].

This claim that the Quaker movement is nothing 'but a spiritual experiment upon the soul' is, I think, a marvellous description of what was, and is, unique about this movement. It is an understanding of life and a way of living life that is based securely in experience, so that its truth and validity can be tested by taking the practical steps required. In this respect then it is less like the truth of the 'witness' in court and more like the truth of the scientist, where the experiment can be run again and again, with many different variations, in order to get closer to the truth. But whereas the scientist can present their findings to the public, or at least to the scientific community, as a basis for their acceptance of the theory, we cannot do this in the field of the spirit. Each of us has to find the truth for ourselves, because the truth always concerns us, in the first instance, and because it relates to that invisible dimension of our existence which we can only be aware of inwardly. That is the Quaker testimony, of course, and if others cannot believe it, let them try the experiment themselves; let them sit in silence and be open to the experience that that makes possible.

3. We can, finally, exhibit the truth in our lives. This is perhaps the most distinctive feature of Quaker communication, but also the most subtle and difficult to describe. It arises from the recognition that words are very limited in expressing and evoking the kind of truth we are concerned with. Consider this advice from George Fox:

> This is to you all that are in the light... that they that act contrary to the light and believe not in it, who know not the word and will not be won with the word (speaking to them), that your chaste conversation (ye walking in the light which comes from the word) may answer to the light in them, which they hate and walk contrary to; that your chaste conversation may judge them and ye may win them.[94]

I'll translate that long sentence into modern English:

> Here's something for all of you who live in the light... when people act contrary to the light and don't believe in it, when they know nothing of the word and won't by won over by the word, that is your speaking to them, then it's down to your pure way of life, that is your acting according to the light that

comes from the word, to evoke the light in them, which they themselves have rejected and refused to follow. Your pure way of life might then show them what they are doing and win them over.

Fox is suggesting, quite remarkably, that even when people are hostile to what Friends say (and not just bemused by it) Friends may nevertheless persuade them to think otherwise by the way they live their lives. How is this possible? This is such an important, and elusive, point we need to give it some further thought.

The witness of life

This is the form of witness we have made especially our own, since it corresponds most closely to the spiritual path we have chosen. Others live impressive, good lives, of course, and they may 'testify' to their profound faith. But Quaker witness is a bit closer than that. We do not witness primarily to our faith, but to truth. We are not trying to demonstrate what we believe or even *that* we believe by living up to what we say we believe, though all these things may happen. The essential thing is that *what we bear witness to is exhibited in our lives*, without anything having to be said.

This is possible because the truth we are concerned with, as we have seen many times, is the reality we experience in our lives, which is mostly too deep, too intimate, too elusive, and yet also too down-to-earth to be adequately expressed in words. But further, we have found that we can get a firmer grasp of this truth, this insight into ourselves and our world, by acting on it. Indeed, if we don't live out in our everyday lives the insights we gain in silent waiting, we will lose the insights and the benefit they bring with them. So we are committed already, for our own benefit, to living consistently with our deepest understanding of truth. This is our joy and our 'life'. We do not have to think how this way of life might benefit others; it might even come as a surprise to us that it has benefitted others. A Quaker life, lived authentically, will be spontaneous and natural, a response to inner 'promptings of love and truth', and not a self-conscious attempt to live according to a set standard. But the inevitable result of living such a way is that other people will notice this and be impressed by it, whether as a good thing to be sought for themselves or as a bad thing to be avoided at all costs.

The most obvious way in which others will be impressed is that they will sense a consistency and closeness between what is said by Friends and what is done by them. They will sense these people are being real, as we now say. If Friends set a fair price for their goods, as they did at the beginning and against the general trend, or if they are straight with people, whoever they are and whatever the issue, if they deal with others as always human and therefore always worthy of respect, people will recognize this as an option for living, even if previously they had thought such a thing was practically impossible. Most people are committed to the idea that to be 'realistic' in life you must not be too 'real'! Quaker lives, lived authentically, challenge that assumption. They tell people that to be fully human, to live out their full potential as human beings and to promote a truly human society, they *must* be real. It is the necessary condition. But this is not an idea put forward as a proposal. It is a lived reality. It will have its impact on people, not because they agree with it, but because, even if they don't agree with it, they will know in their hearts it is a fact of life to be reckoned with.

George Fox gives a good example of such an impact from his own experience. I will give it in a modern form; you can find the original in his *Journal*:[95]

After the meeting was over and I had gone up to my room, another ambassador arrived at Pall Mall with a company of Irish colonels, a rough bunch of men. I heard one of them say he would kill all the Quakers, and the Baptists, Presbyterians, Independents and Monarchy people. So I went down to him and I was moved by the power of the Lord to say something to him, and it obviously took hold of him. I said, 'The *law* said "an eye for an eye and a tooth for a tooth", but you threatened to kill the Quakers and others though they have done you no harm. Well, here is *gospel* for you: here is my hair, here is my cheek, and here are my shoulders', and I turned them towards him. He and his company were so amazed by this that they said if that was our basis and we lived by what we said, then they never saw the like in their lives. So I told them all that I was the same in life as I was in words, and the truth so took hold of him that he grew to be loving.[96]

That last sentence reads in Fox's own words:

So I told him and them I was the same in life as I was in words, and the truth came so over him that he grew loving.

What is surprising in this story is that the 'truth' which 'came so over him' was not in what Fox had said, but in what he had done. He had explained his action, certainly, but the ambassador was only asking to have his impression confirmed. So Fox confirmed that what he did in 'turning his cheek', literally, came from the heart and corresponded to what he had said about the 'law' and the 'gospel'. Moreover, this truth, which came from Fox's heart and was expressed in his action, touched the heart of the ambassador and transformed his hostility into love. He had been 'won over', in words from the earlier quotation, by Fox's manner of life. Fox's action corresponded with what he, the ambassador, knew in his heart to be true, and in recognizing that and accepting that he discovered his own true self and his own real feeling; hence his gratitude to Fox. And all this seems to have happened in a matter of minutes!

This then is how testimony works when it takes the form of a human life. It expresses the reality that Friends have known in their own experience by their living in harmony with it, and that lived expression of truth then resonates with what other people know in themselves, even if they do not themselves live by this truth. The lived testimony then has the effect of arousing the sense of reality that they have repressed or denied, and it challenges them to take it seriously. It gives them a new choice: they can embrace this truth, now that it is offered again, or they can reject it and return to the ideas and beliefs by which they lived previously. The 'witness of life' works, when it does work, by 'answering that of God' in other people. This should help to explain that famous passage of Fox where he urged Friends to carry their message in this rather unique way wherever they went in the world:

Be patterns, be examples in all countries, places, islands, nations, wherever you come, that your carriage and life may preach among all sorts of people, and to them. Then you will come to walk cheerfully over the world, answering that of God in every one, whereby in them ye may be a blessing and make the witness of God in them to bless you.[97]

The testimonies

It was possible therefore to describe the whole of someone's life as a 'testimony'. Isaac Penington went to jail, he says, 'for his testimony to truth', that is, for his refusal to do or say anything false, whatever the consequences. But the word also came to apply to specific actions, or to specific kinds of action, which Friends generally felt would bear witness to the truth of their situation. The most famous testimony in this sense was and has been the peace testimony. But see how it was first described, and compare that with how it is mostly thought of today. It was articulated first when the king returned to rule in 1660 and Friends were concerned he might suspect the Friends of plotting against him – there were groups who were doing this, like the Fifth Monarchists, and Friends were already being tarred with the same brush:

> Our principle is, and our practices have always been, to seek peace and ensue it and to follow after righteousness and the knowledge of God, seeking the good and welfare and doing that which tends to the peace of all. We know that wars and fightings proceed from the lusts of men (as Jas. iv.1-3), out of which lusts the Lord hath redeemed us, and so out of the occasion of war. The occasion of which war, and war itself (wherein envious men, who are lovers of themselves more than lovers of God, lust, kill and desire to have men's lives or estates) ariseth from the lust. All bloody principles and practices, we, as to our own particulars, do utterly deny, with all outward wars and strife and fightings with outward weapons, for any end or under any pretence whatsoever. And this is our testimony to the whole world... We whom the Lord hath called into the obedience of his truth have denied wars and fightings and cannot again any more learn of it. This is a certain testimony unto all the world of the truth of our hearts in this particular, that as God persuadeth every man's heart to believe, so they may receive it.[98]

What was their testimony to? Not the value of peace, or their belief that war was wrong, as we tend to express it today. They were testifying to 'the truth of our hearts in this particular,' what they knew from experience about the reality of war and violent conflict. Many of them had lived and even fought in the Civil War, and they knew of the appalling destructiveness and futility of war. They had seen through the illusion that war can achieve humane ends like liberty and peace. It rather sows the seeds of further conflict by creating bitterness and the desire for revenge.

They also knew that it arose in the first place from the similar 'passions' of hatred and greed, that is, selfish desires that see other people as either a means or a hindrance to their own fulfilment. So long as people are driven by such selfish desire they will continue to struggle in this way and continue to cause suffering to themselves and others. They do not see their connectedness with other humans but imagine they are separate and need to fend for themselves. This false understanding feeds their desire, and their desire further blinds them to the consequences of what they do. But Friends have been delivered from this desire by being enabled, by the light of Christ within them, to see the truth. So they see clearly the evil of violence - the futility of forcing their will on others or punishing them - for any purpose whatever, and therefore refuse to deploy it. This action, this refusal to use violence for their own purposes, is itself their testimony to the reality of violence. They hope, in conclusion, that others, especially the king, will be so touched in their hearts by this action that they will 'receive' the Friends' testimony and embrace it themselves.

We can learn from this example that the specific actions that Friends undertook as a testimony to the truth, as they saw it, were directed at specific evils of their time. They were concerted responses to evils that pervaded their society and brought about much misery. Fox made a point of this in one of his rare descriptions of what testimonies are:

> Be faithful in your testimonies of life and light, against all those things which have come up in this night of apostasy from the light, life and power of God.[99]

'This night of apostasy' refers to that long time of darkness when people could not see clearly, when, having lost 'the light, life and power' which had been given them by God with the coming of Jesus, they had to picture the world to themselves as their own desires fashioned it. They invented structures of ideas that would make sense of the world and structures of power that would ensure they got what they wanted. Since all this was done in ignorance of what people really needed, i.e. the truth about humans, it caused them much suffering. So now Friends were called to bring their new-found 'light and life' to bear on this miserable situation and help people to see what they had been doing, and what had been done to them.

These characteristic actions or behaviours have sometimes been grouped together so that we can understand them more clearly, and recognize their continuing relevance today. This was first done, I believe, by the Quaker historian Hugh Barbour in his *The Quakers in Puritan England*. He grouped them under four headings, equality, simplicity, honesty and peace. That grouping is still valid, though a fifth testimony is sometimes added, community, which deals with the Quaker alternatives to the ritualized control of community life, and a sixth is in the process of emerging, namely a testimony of care for the earth, but I will not write about them here[100] .

1. **Equality** is the practice of treating people with equal regard, since they are discerned to be of one family, one race. They may pretend to be otherwise, some claiming to be inherently superior, and others meekly accepting this. But this pretence inevitably leads to trouble. In seventeenth century England society was stratified according to this sense of superiority. The king and his lords and bishops had more power, wealth and privilege according to their supposedly greater worth as human beings, or their greater endowment by God; those who had much less, or virtually nothing, were supposed to accept this state of affairs as their lot. This huge disparity, and the suffering and misery that went with it, was one of the causes of the Civil War. Now the Quakers, who had witnessed all this for themselves and at some time been driven to despair by it, began to see through it all. This

is what the Light within them was doing for them. So they protested against it in the name of reality, i.e. they bore witness to the truth, and they did so primarily by treating their fellow humans *as* fellow humans, addressing their supposed superiors with the familiar word 'thou', offering them a handshake rather than bowing and scraping before them and doffing their hat, and other such pointed actions. This may have caused offence, of course, but it was not intended for that purpose; it was intended to communicate a simple truth, which often it did. Today, we have to find, and do find, different sorts of action which nevertheless convey the same basic truth about human equality and human solidarity.

2. **Simplicity** follows directly and naturally from the concern for equality and justice. It is about living a life that makes for harmony between human beings rather than discord and conflict. Because resources are limited, especially now with a much expanded population, we cannot possess all that we might want without depriving others of what they need. So we live according to our needs, rather than our wants. This in any case is truthful living and healthy living, freeing us from the clutter and anxiety that go with many possessions. But it also communicates to others the idea of living without the many things that our culture likes to think are desirable. In the beginning that meant wearing a simple set of clothes, not unlike a poorly paid worker might wear – clothes 'with a working class accent,' as Barbour puts it – not because that was an aesthetic ideal, but in order to express solidarity with those who had little. Listen to James Nayler from those early days:

> Is this the Saints' practice... to live in the lusts of the flesh, sporting and gaming and calling it 'recreation,' living in excess of apparel and diet... when your brethren want food and rayment?[101]

Today, it touches on our ownership of houses, cars and fashionable clothes, as well as on our spending on travel, leisure and entertainment.

3. Honesty is an obvious expression of truth. It implies that we face the truth in ourselves and express that truth in our communication with others. This was particularly important at the beginning when it was generally felt that honesty could be dangerous or misleading, and that it was better to say what was acceptable by the standards of the church or state. Their concern to be always 'theologically correct' has a certain parallel in our more secular age with 'political correctness', which can also inhibit honesty and truthfulness. Behind it is the fear of being judged unacceptable by others, rather than a positive concern to help others. Honesty had another meaning in the market place. Trade was generally undertaken by bargaining; you gained the highest possible price for what you sold, and the lowest possible price for what you bought. In the forefront of your trading was your own personal interest. Quakers denounced the practice as untruthful, and open to exploitation, but more importantly they insisted in being honest in their own business practice. They decided what an article was worth, and stuck to that value in their buying or selling it. They more or less invented the price tag. But this principle of 'acting the truth', as George Fox called it, extended more widely. It meant that you kept by your promise, honoured the person you were dealing with, took account of the interests of all those involved, whatever your trade or profession. So Quakers became trusted as bankers, for example, because they would look after people's money. We would now call this **integrity,** rather than simply honesty, and I think this is now a better description of this cluster of testimonies. Integrity is what we need when we face the complexities of modern business and trade, and the universal tendency in all use of money to deceive in the interest of personal gain.

4. **Peace**, as we have seen, is not so much a witness to the value of peace as a practice of peace-making that bears witness to the truth about violence and conflict in human relations. It is telling people what they know in their hearts about the reality of violence, but are afraid to accept because violence appears, in the short term, to solve so many problems. It appears to destroy the enemy, to force people to act in the way we deem to be right, and to overcome conflict and make for peace. In fact it does none of these things. Our dependence on violence is based on an illusion, which serves only to comfort us as we face the pain of conflict or the discomfort of our guilt at using others for our own advantage. Talking to people about the futility of such actions seems to have little effect. Treating people with respect and affection even while we are in conflict with them, refusing to hurt them with physical or psychological force, can penetrate their minds more deeply and dispel the illusion. The refusal of Friends in the twentieth century to fight in our wars has had a huge effect over the years in shaping people's perception of war, which is seen now less as a glorious act of patriotism and more as a necessary evil.

I hope enough has been said to clarify these distinctly Quaker responses to the evils in our world in the hope of communicating what Quakers have discovered of the reality of our life as humans. These testimonies speak, not of ideals that we hope to put in to practice and encourage others to do the same, but of the reality that underlies our social ills so that others may recognize it and live their lives accordingly. They are pointers, protests, pleas for change. But whether such practices are effective and can make a real difference to the world is altogether another question. This will be our theme for our next and final chapter.

Chapter seven

Changing Things

Our final theme is 'changing things', which Quakers have been very obviously concerned about from the beginning of their history. But why? The reason may not be immediately apparent from observing their behaviour in meeting for worship. They seem, at first glance, to be inward-looking, content with the sustenance they gain from sitting quietly in worship. Many other groups, with a similar contemplative approach to life, express little interest in the world and may even try to avoid it altogether. How come Quakers are different?

Let's look a little more deeply into Quaker practice and we should see an answer to this question, and this in turn will help us to see also *how* they go about changing things. For there's no doubt that our unusual practice of looking for the truth in silence has a profound effect on the way we engage with other people.

Feeling

The point of sitting in the silence, as we have seen, is first of all to see things more clearly. We are very aware that our view of things can be clouded by selfish interest or anxiety. Indeed, we can get locked into a concern for ourselves which prevents us seeing anything clearly. We are then living in the dark, or at least, in a murky twilight in which it is hard to discern what is going on around us. This is when we make mistakes, sometimes very big mistakes, and this is when we might shake ourselves and say 'What am I doing with my life?' Sitting quietly for a time with an open mind and heart might enable the answer to emerge. A Light within us will enable us to see ourselves and what we are doing. It might even show us, if we are open and receptive enough, that it is the self that gets in the way. But this 'self' which we are so concerned to protect is not our real self, we find; it is an idea that we and others have constructed. Insofar as we think it *is* real it is a false self! But if we recognize this fact, we will discover something much deeper in us that we have not created, our true self: what we are really, and what we are meant to be. We call it the spirit or 'the seed' (the old Quaker language) or the Christ within. If we accept that as our true self, letting go all images and ideas about what we are, we will experience a connectedness with life which is astonishingly fresh and invigorating, and perhaps a connection with the ultimate source of life (as I discussed in my second chapter). But there is also the feeling, which may take time to grow, of closeness with other people, a feeling of belonging, of being 'bound up in the bundle of love and life,' as Elizabeth Bathurst put it.[102] Other people are no longer strangers, aliens, who have nothing to do with us. They are kith and kin, so to speak. As a result we can begin to feel for them and sympathize with them, without this feeling always being checked and chained by our worry for ourselves. This is love in the spiritual sense.

And love, in the spiritual sense, is what inspires and motivates us to help other people. It is a quite natural response, a 'prompting of love and truth in our hearts'. If others are in pain, we feel some pain too. If others are in need, we want to help. None of this is adequate, of course, for dealing with the complex situations we all get into, but it is a start. And for us Quakers it is *the* start. As John Woolman said, back in the eighth-teenth century, describing how he got to be concerned with the American Indians:

> Love was the first motion, and then a concern arose to spend some time with the Indians, that I might feel and understand their life, and the Spirit they live in, if haply I might receive some instruction from them, or they be in any degree helped forward by my following the leadings of Truth amongst them.

And as it pleased the Lord to make way for my going at a time when the troubles of war were increasing and when by reason of much wet weather travelling was more difficult than usual at that season, I looked upon it as a more favourable opportunity to season my mind, and bring me into a nearer sympathy with them. And as mine eye was to the great Father of Mercies, humbly desiring to learn what his will was concerning me, I was made quiet and content.[103]

This may sound innocent enough as a starting point, even obvious, so let me underline the consequences. It means that we do not seek to change things out of anger, or pride, or a desire to prove ourselves right or worthy. These are very common motivations for change, which we must all be familiar with, but they lead to quite different results. If you are angry about a state of affairs, for example, you will want to find who is to blame; that person or system, or whatever is responsible, then becomes your enemy. To change the world for the better you have to destroy the enemy. On the other hand, if you are motivated by pride – 'See what I can do!' - or its obverse, a feeling of worthlessness, you will do things that will draw attention to yourself, and you will want to make the people around you feel *less* worthy than you are. In this competitive situation they are not likely to give of their best, and neither are you. But these desires are what we all have to deal with, and we can deal with them if we allow our real motivations to come to light. We can then 'take heed... to the promptings of love and truth' without distraction. Our waiting in silence is then, in part, a purification of desire.

Understanding

When we have tested our motives, however, and found a situation that calls for our help, we will soon find that a right concern is not always enough. Love is not always all you need! To take the simplest illustrations: we may want to help someone who has fallen down on the rocky path, but if we do the immediately obvious thing and help them to get up we could make matters worse. They may have broken a bone or been concussed. In that case they have to be allowed to rest where they are until a stretcher can be brought. Again, we may give money to a beggar in the street because we think he needs food or clothing; in fact he may be looking for his next fix or can of cider. Anthony de Mello has a good story about our eagerness to help. A priest saw a small boy in the street trying to reach the high knocker on a front door. The priest went up to the door and rapped the knocker loudly for him. 'What do we do now?', he said to the boy. 'Run like hell!' he said.

We need to understand people before we can help them, but understanding may not always be easy to come by. People's difficulties may be hidden. They are usually complex and often intractable – people get stuck in situations with no obvious way out, like poverty or addiction. So an effort has to be made to understand their whole situation. Remember what Woolman said after he described his being moved to help the Indians. 'Love was the first motion, and then a concern arose to spend some time with the Indians, that I might feel and understand their life'.

This is widely recognized, of course. In the modern outlook in particular it is emphasized that we need to use reason in a fairly systematic way to understand the complex. Science has been used very much for this purpose. Where we face a group of people in need, we can rely on scientists, usually social or psychological scientists, to give us an 'analysis' of what is going on. They can draw on large theories which have been drawn up from the study of the 'data'. This can be very helpful. Poverty, for example, can be seen to be maintained by the economic system, even when attempts are made by charities, or even by government, to alleviate it. We then understand that poverty cannot be overcome until we change the economic system. But how do you do that? And what alternative system would be realistically possible as well as actually desirable?

Here the social scientist or economist is soon out of their depth. For these are questions about people and how they act and interact. So to answer these question moderns tend to resort to ideology, that is, to a system of ideas which explains the whole of human life in a way that protects what we take to be important and worthwhile in human life. More traditional people might turn to theology for their answers, that is, to a system of ideas based on the authority of a tradition or a sacred text. These ideas cannot be grounded in experience in the way science is, because they are meant to provide the *whole picture*, which is beyond our experience. Ideologies and theologies tend therefore to be dogmatic, unable to verify their stances, and unable to communicate effectively with anybody who disagrees with them. This is true of communists and capitalists, as much as Christian or Muslim fundamentalists.

This is not true, however, and cannot be true of Quakers. They do not have the whole picture, and cannot have it, precisely because their understanding is based on experience and committed to it. Like Paul the Apostle, they 'know in part and prophesy in part'.[104] Although they may 'see things as they are', beginning with how they themselves are, the things they see are limited to their particular situation. They need other people, with different perspectives, to see things more fully. Even then, they will not see the whole; they will see that part of the world that presents itself to them. But if they are thorough and patient enough in their discipline, they will see enough to know how they are to act, and how to act effectively.

The word normally used for this discipline is 'discernment'. This conveys the idea that the understanding is reached by bringing many factors together:

what we know objectively of the facts of the situation,

what we variously perceive the situation to be,

what the people in the situation have to say about it (or otherwise express by their behaviour),

what we sense or feel is going on as we 'wait in the light',

what we know from our experiences of situations like this, some of which goes very deep into our life.

The discernment is the sense of what is really going on, that answers what we felt initially to be in need of help or some other intervention. As the discernment is formulated in words to be shared among all concerned, it will be checked by those concerned, and then tested in experience as the understanding is put into action. Since there is no ideology here, no official doctrine, the understanding can be changed in the light of new experience, a new turn of events, and the action altered accordingly. It is a fluid, flexible and responsive process, enabling everyone involved to respond consciously to the situation as they perceive it. It exemplifies that fundamental commitment in the Quaker way, that truth, as each can know it for themselves, is what ultimately enables us to live freely and fully.

If this process can be made effective in the larger issues of the world, it shows that the Quaker way, though starting always with the individual, opens out fairly soon to others and to the complex relations in which they have to live.

'This light which is of God', wrote Fox, 'lets thee see all the works of the world',[105] just as it had let them see what they were doing themselves. William Penn wrote a similar thing in his long Preface to Fox's *Journal* (see full passage in Appendix 5), but it also describes how the Quakers understood the world and were led to try and change it. He was a refined and educated man himself, and his first encounter with the Quakers, who on the whole were not then refined or highly educated, may be reflected in his description of their behaviour:

These things [their living with ruthless honesty and simplicity] to be sure gave them a rough and disagreeable appearance with the generality, who thought them turners of the world upside down, as indeed in some sense they were, but in no other than that wherein Paul was so charged, viz. to bring things back into their primitive and right order again. For these and such like practices of theirs were not the result of humour, or for civil distinction, as some have fancied, but a fruit of inward sense, which God, through his holy fear, had begotten in them. They did not consider how to contradict the world, or distinguish themselves as a party from others, it being none of their business, as it was not their interest. No, it was not the result of consultation, or a framed design, by which to declare or recommend schism or novelty. But God having given them a sight of themselves, they saw the whole world in the same glass of truth, and sensibly discerned the affections and passions of men, and the rise and tendency of things.[106]

You notice the phrase 'they... sensibly discerned' what others were feeling and doing, implying that the Quakers could see beyond the obvious facts and forces at work to the deeper motivations of people. But what is most striking is *how* they were able to do this. They could see others clearly because they had first been 'given a sight of themselves'. God had given them a mirror, a 'glass', to show them the truth, and having looked in the mirror and seen themselves (!), they could then turn the mirror slightly to see the rest of the world. They could recognize what was really going on for others, because they had discovered these very feelings and motivations in themselves. It is also interesting *what* they saw, or 'discerned': 'the affections and passions of men, the rise and tendency of things'. They did not see impersonal systems, of church and state e.g., or mythological powers like Satan and demons, though these were the concern of many of their contemporaries. They saw *people*, and the feelings that motivated them. And the basic feeling they saw in them was a desire to possess and to be seen to possess, as Penn continues: 'what it was that gratified the lust of the flesh, the lust of the eye and the pride of life'. He is quoting James here, from the New Testament, but we must be careful not to read 'the lust of the flesh' in a narrowly sexual sense. The phrase at the time referred to all the desires that spring from a self-centred view of life, 'the flesh' being the merely human aspect of ourselves, contrasted with the spirit. Friends saw wars arising from 'the passions and lusts of the flesh' (as in the Peace Declaration, already quoted, and in Appendix 4), that is, the desire to gain material wealth, or to protect the wealth one had. They saw injustice arising from 'the pride of life', which meant, I think, a pride in being superior to others and therefore not having to give others a fair share.

Now all these powerful desires arise, says Penn, 'in the night of darkness and apostasy, which hath been over people through their degeneration from the light and spirit of God'. What does that mean? 'The night of darkness' was a standard image of the time for ignorance, lack of awareness.[107] 'Darkness' is the state of not being able to see. So Penn is saying that people behave in the selfish and destructive way they do because they cannot really see the situation in which they live. Being unaware of their connectedness with other human beings and with God, they feel free to abuse them. But more that that, being unaware of this connection they feel isolated and alone, bonded only perhaps with their family and friends. But they know they depend on others for survival, so they are in constant struggle to get hold of what they need (or perceive that they need), whatever the cost to others. That darkness (you see) is the source of the evil they do. And how could they do otherwise? you might ask.

This is a bleak view of the world, it has to be said. The source of trouble in the world is seen to be in the way humans are both with themselves and with others. To change the world for the better we have to change people, or rather, we have to learn to act in a way that will help people to change. So Penn rejects all social and political plans or 'designs' for this purpose, since they fail to get to the core of the problem. He insists on understanding *why* people behave as they do.

But notice the flipside. If people would be enabled to 'see' better, they would naturally behave better. They would see through their self-centredness as a kind of stupidity, and they would recognise other people as humans like themselves. That means that humans are not essentially bad or selfish. Nor are they trapped by evil or 'sin', as was generally thought in the seventeenth century. They are capable of feeling and behaving differently. It also means that Quakers cannot see themselves as superior to others, and they cannot 'judge' others as 'bad people'. Rather, they see a deep connection with people, a solidarity even, even when others are behaving badly. Or we could say, especially when they are behaving badly, because Quakers (who are honest) will recognise that they do behave, or have behaved, in much the same sort of way. Jesus is supposed to have said about the men who nailed him to a cross, 'Father, forgive them, for they know not what they do'.

Faith

Friends can take this cool view of evil in the world because they have discovered something in themselves that enables them to overcome it. Evil and sin have lost their power. Violence and oppression and greed, which arise out of darkness, are vulnerable to the light. In the light we can see that they are all misplaced, futile and unproductive. They do not produce the goods they promise, and they do not, finally, satisfy those who perpetrate them. It is mistaken to see these destructive things as the 'hard realities' of life. They are real, of course, in the sense that they exist. But they are not based on a realistic under-standing of life. On the contrary, they arise from the illusory view that 'we' are alone in the world and have to fight against the world to maintain ourselves. This is a dream, or even a nightmare. In order to connect with reality and find a real life we have to wake up from this dream and learn to see and touch and feel the world as it is.

There is a line in a novel by Nikos Kazantzakis, *Report to Greco* (really an autobiography), which raises this question about what is real in the world. He walks out onto the streets of Berlin at the end of the First World War. It is a Sunday morning, and mist hangs about with the dust in the streets, and he says: 'Behind the mist I observed the world, half solid, half composed of dreams'.[108]

That, surprisingly, is a source of hope for Friends. Listen to Penn again, from the first paragraph of the extract I've given. The early Quakers, he says:

> adhere to this blessed light in themselves, which discovers and condemns sin in all its appearances *and shows how to overcome it,* if minded and obeyed in its holy manifestations and convictions, *giving power to such to avoid and resist* those things that do not please God, and to grow strong in love, faith and good works.[109]

Václav Havel was not a Quaker, but he had a way of thinking and feeling that echoes the Quaker sensibility, and shows what it might mean in a modern, political context. In a famous essay from prison, 'The power of the powerless', he gives an account of the resistance to the Communist regime in Czechoslovakia in the 1970s, the movement that eventually led to the overthrow of the regime and the liberation of the country in 1989. He calls the resistance 'living in truth'. The real resistance to evil, he argues, does not take place in the battle of ideologies, in the use of arms or wealth or social power, but in what he calls the 'hidden sphere of truth':

If the main pillar of the system is living a lie, then it is not surprising that the fundamental threat to it is living the truth. That is why it must be suppressed more severely than anything else...

How does the power of truth operate?...

Under the orderly surface of the life of lies... there slumbers the hidden sphere of life in its real aims, of its hidden openness to truth... The effective range of this special power [of truth] cannot be measured in terms of disciples, voters or soldiers, because it lies spread out in the fifth column of social consciousness, in the hidden aims of life, in human beings' repressed longing for dignity and fundamental rights, for the realization of their real social and political interests.[110]

It is not our responsibility to take control of the situation, or even of a part of it. We are not ourselves going to change the world. We can only link in with this hidden sphere of truth, and truth itself will change things.

We have seen how this operates at the personal level in a story about George Fox.[111] When he was threatened by some Irish colonels who wanted to 'kill all the Quakers' he 'turned his other cheek' towards them and said, 'Strike me then'. This so affected their leader, 'the truth came so over him', as Fox puts it, that his hostility was changed to love. It was Fox acting out his truth, presenting his humanity to the colonels which they had failed to recognize, that enabled the soldiers to see the reality. It is doubtful if Fox would have been able persuade them of this by merely arguing with them (which he did on other occasions, of course, and not to great effect). It is seeing the truth lived out that makes the difference, because this penetrates beneath the surface of words and defences and excuses. We have also seen that that was the power of the Quaker 'testimonies'. As practical embodiments of truth they touch that depth in people's hearts where they know the truth, even when they are denying it with the top of their heads. So the witness to truth turns out to be an effective way of changing things as well.

It is important, though, that actions exemplifying the truth should not be felt as aggressive or over-critical. The early Quakers did not always take this to heart. In their eagerness to wake people up from their 'dreams', they often provoked them and alienated them. Alexander Parker mourned this fact in a letter to George Fox in 1660, when the Quakers were in danger of a more intense persecution by the State than they had experienced already. 'Better had it been if all had been kept still and quiet in those times, for because of the forwardness and want of wisdom in some is one great cause of our present sufferings'.[112] From that time on they were in fact more gentle and peaceable, as their Peace Declaration of the same year promised. They found a way to express the love they felt for others, even as they protested against the way they were living. This combination of love and truth, of gentleness and firmness, has the effect of opening both the heart and the mind. It can establish dialogue and mutual understanding, where previously there might have been misunderstanding and distrust. That is another reason then why Quakers are committed to nonviolence. Violence not only hurts people we care for, and degrades people whom we recognise as God's children too, it also shuts their eyes and their ears. It provokes resistance, resentment and bitterness, which of course make matters worse in the long run, even if it succeeds in making a gain in the short run. Nonviolence is therefore perceived by Quakers to be, not so much an ideal we hope others will admire, as a realistic response to the problems of human conflict and oppression that makes a real difference.

Action

Finally, when Friends are challenged by a situation that concerns them and they have checked out their motivation for getting involved, when they have sought to understand what is really happening there so that they can know how to act appropriately, and when they have attempted in one way or another to communicate the truth they have discerned, they can then take action to provide real help. Let me give an example.

In 1813 Elizabeth Fry was taken around Newgate Prison in London by a friend of hers. She was appalled. It was overcrowded and filthy. The prisoners were underfed, uncared for and morally degraded. Elizabeth Fry was moved to do something. But first she wanted to learn what was going on in the prison, especially among the women prisoners. She visited them and talked with them at length to understand their situation. And being a woman of some social standing – from one of the rich banking families in the country, the Gurneys – she was able to talk to the governor of the prison and members of parliament. The situation became clear. The prisoners were thought of as less than human. They were being punished by the State in the desperate attempt to rid them of their evil intent, and to deter anyone else like them who might consider doing similar things. But Elizabeth Fry discovered that this was a gross misjudgement, both of the people who were being ill-treated in prison and of the effects such a punitive regime would have on them. In fact no serious attempt had been made to understand these people. No one really listened to them. They were being treated on the basis of preconceived ideas and prejudices in a spirit of revenge and hatred. Fry realized she had to act in such a way as to highlight their humanity and communicate the truth of what was happening here. This she did, visiting the prisoners regularly, helping them with practical necessities, organizing sewing classes that could earn them money, and teaching them to read and understand the Bible. Her action drew attention to what was happening in the prison. Prominent Victorians came to the prison just to see this well-to-do, respectable woman fraternizing with criminals. It had a big effect, and soon a movement was afoot to reform the whole prison system and treat criminals with respect.

A modern example of a typical intervention can be found at the Quaker offices at the United Nations in Geneva and New York. Not much is known about them because their work is deliberately low-key, and indeed confidential. What they are doing is to bring politicians and diplomats together so that they can really listen to one another, without the pressure of the media glare, and get to know one another and their various concerns and constraints. Friends had been supportive of the United Nations from the beginning, but they noticed that its activities were being hampered by a lack of understanding between the countries that found themselves at odds. The problem was not that their interests really conflicted, but that they were perceived to conflict because of the way the politicians had been led to think about one another. Meetings were therefore arranged so that a genuine understanding, and respect, could be established.[113] In this way Friends have been able to facilitate mediation between countries that were in serious conflict, for example between Israel and Egypt in 1956, and in the Biafran War of the 1970s.[114]

It can be seen however, that a good part of the action in such interventions is getting people to listen and to understand. This was brought home to me when I attended a lecture on the anti-slavery movement, at the time that the two-hundreth anniversary of the abolition of the slave trade was being celebrated in 2007. The lecturer, James Walvin, who was an expert on the history of slavery, made the point that behind the success of Wilberforce in parliament was a Committee of twelve people who had campaigned throughout England in the previous decades. Moreover, nine of these twelve people were Quakers. I asked him a question at the end of the lecture – I wrote it down afterwards, I was so impressed by his reply – 'You have described the huge impact the Quakers had on the abolition movement in the late eighteenth century. But they had a very different ethic from most people in the country. How did they manage to persuade people that slavery was wrong?' He replied: 'It was surprisingly simple. The Quakers told people what exactly was happening. They told them the truth'. [115]

So once again we notice how close these two concerns are: to communicate the truth and to help relieve suffering. The most effective way of our communicating the truth that is of most concern to us is to live it out in our lives. Our lives become our testimony. We now see that in seeking to relieve suffering the most effective means we have is to convey the truth of the situation that causes suffering. We have confidence that people have the resources within them, maybe deep within them and unknown to themselves, to recognize the realities of their life and to respond with an open heart. There is no guarantee that they will, of course. And we have no control over how people inwardly respond to situations; nor does anyone else. We can only trust the secret processes at work in people, and hope that they come to fruition. That hope is based, not on any dogma, but on what we ourselves have experienced of those secret processes, and on what we see happening in those around us. It is perhaps a slender hope, compared with the grand schemes and plans that others may trust in, but we are confident that it is very well grounded, and that it is enough to inspire us to work for a good outcome.

Appendix I

Hidden or Veiled Spiritual Verities Revealed

Samuel Fisher, 1661[116]

Query 1. What is God really in himself, without any definition? And in what did he dwell, and manifest himself before the foundation of the heavens and the earth was laid?

Answer 1. God, as he is really in himself, is beyond all definition of ours at all... but, if speaking by way of such description as those have made of him, who have seen and known him... I answer, God (whatever more he is, that's nothing to us)... is really in himself, whatever he hath at any time, in and by his son, revealed himself to be, in and to his holy prophets, and children; and whatever they in all ages (as moved by him so to do) have declared him to be, whether by word of mouth or scripture. And so whatever ye there read God is, that God is really, indeed and in truth, (viz.) a spirit, light, love, that one, omnipotent, all-sufficient, spiritual, substantial, living, everlasting, infinite subsistence, which hath his own being of himself and gives being, life, breath and all things unto all, in whom we and all mankind, who are his offspring, both live, move and have our being.

Howbeit, there is not in every man, no not in all those that read of him there, and can speak of him what they there read, the true knowledge of him so... For they only truly know him to be this or that, who witness him truly to be this or that to and within themselves. And those know him not... that prate this and that of him like [mag]pies and parrots, which may be taught... yet come not to find and feel him so to be... in his own light, by which he draws nigh to, and is not far from every one of us. By which [light]... in some measure, though not the same measure, he manifests something of himself in every conscience... and to such as love him and keep his commandments given out in the same, he manifests himself in such wise as he will not do to the world. Yea, in such wise that they can experientally say... that God is, and that he is true, good, merciful, faithful, just, righteous in taking vengeance; that he is a judge, a protector, a saviour, a redeemer... Whereas therefore ye query, What God really is in himself? As God saith of himself, I am that I am; so say I, *Deus est id quod est:* God is what he is; and if ye, who by your asking of us, profess yourselves to be yet ignorant of him... would know him in any measure, as he really is in himself, my counsel to you is, to stand still in his own counsel, namely, his light in your own consciences, that in that you may be led forth into his life and likeness, even into the image of his son, the light of the world, the righteous, pure, meek, innocent, gentle, loving, peaceable, inoffensive, merciful, compassionate, tender, patient lamb of God, that takes away the sin of it, who is the express image of the Father... Wait for his appearing in his own spirit and power to restore his own image in your hearts, that as he appeareth, ye may appear with him in his glory, which is fulness of grace and truth, being transformed into his image from glory to glory, by the operation of his holy spirit, that as he appeareth, ye may be like him, and so see him as he is.

Query 2. Whether is there a manifestation of God in everything that hath a life, motion and being in this outward creation? And whether is a creature to expect ever to know God under any other dispensation or administration, further than by the manifestation of the Spirit of God in him...

Answer 2. This second query stands in two parts, to the first of which I answer, Yes, as 'tis said, *Deo plena sunt omnia: Est Deus in nobis, agitante calescimus ipso* [All things are full of God, God is in us, we grow warm by his own moving; from Ovid's *Fasti*, VI.5].

To the second I answer, Nay, there is no other way, dispensation or administration in or under which a creature is to expect to know God, further than by the manifestation of the spirit of God in him; for it is written, Rom.1.19, 'Whatever is to be known of God is manifest in men, for God doth show it in them'.

Appendix 2

The Sense of the Meeting

Quaker Faith and Practice[117]

3.02

In our meetings for worship we seek through the stillness to know God's will for ourselves and for the gathered group. Our meetings for church affairs, in which we conduct our business, are also meeting for worship based on silence, and they carry the same expectation that God's guidance can be discerned if we are truly listening together and to each other, and are not blinkered by preconceived opinions. It is this belief that God's will can be recognized through the discipline of silent waiting which distinguishes our decision-making process from the secular idea of consensus. We have a common purpose in seeking God's will through waiting and listening, believing that every activity of life should be subject to divine guidance.

This does not mean that laughter and a sense of humour should be absent from our meetings for church affairs. It does mean that at all times there should be an inward recollection: out of this will spring a right dignity, flexible and free from pomp and formality. We meet together for common worship, for the pastoral care of our membership, for needful administration, for unhurried deliberations on matters of common concern, for testing personal concerns that are brought before us, and to get to know one another better in things that are eternal as in things that are temporal.

3.03

...We are enjoined to live adventurously, but experiment must be grounded in the experience of generations of Friends, which offers us a method, a purpose and principles for the right conduct of our business meetings...

3.04

Our method of conducting our meetings for church affairs is an experience which has been tested over three hundred years. In days of hot contest and bitter controversy the early Friends, knit together by the glorious experience of the Holy Spirit's guidance in all their affairs, came into the simple understanding of how their corporate decisions should be made.

We have learned to eschew lobbying and not to set great store by rhetoric or clever argument. The mere gaining of debating points is found to be unhelpful and alien to the spirit of worship which should govern the rightly ordered meeting. Instead of rising hastily to reply to another, it is better to give time for what has been said to make its own appeal. We must always be ready to give serious, unhurried and truly sympathetic consideration to proposals brought forward from whatever part of the meeting. We should neither be hindered from making experiments by fear or undue caution, nor prompted by novel suggestions to ill-considered courses.

3.05

The right conduct of our meeting for church affairs depends upon all coming to them in an active, seeking spirit, not with minds already made up on a particular course of action, determined to push this through at all costs. But open minds are not empty minds, nor uncritically receptive: the service of the meeting calls for knowledge of facts, often painstakingly acquired, and the ability to estimate their relevance and importance. This demands that we shall be ready to listen to others carefully, without antagonism if they express opinions which are unpleasing to us, but trying always to discern the truth in what they have to offer. It calls, above all, for spiritual sensitivity. If our meetings fail, the failure may well be in those who are ill-prepared to use the method rather than in the inadequacy of the method itself.

It is always to be recognised that, coming together with a variety of temperaments, of background, education and experience, we shall have differing contributions to make to any deliberations. It is not part of Friends' concern for truth that any should be expected to water down a strong conviction or be silent merely for the sake of easy agreement. Nevertheless we are called to honour our testimony that to everyone is given a measure of the light, and that it is in the sharing of knowledge, experience and concern that the way towards unity will be found. There is need for understanding loyalty by the meeting as a whole when, after all sides of a subject have been considered, a minute is accepted as representing the discernment of the meeting. Not all who attend a meeting for church affairs will necessarily speak: those who are silent can help to develop the sense of the meeting if they listen in a spirit of worship.

3.06

The unity we seek depends on the willingness of us all to seek the truth in each other's utterances; on our being open to persuasion; and in the last resort on a willingness to recognize and accept the sense of the meeting as recorded in the minute, knowing that our dissenting views have been heard and considered. We do not vote in our meetings, because we believe that this would emphasise the divisions between differing views and inhibit the process of seeking to know the will of God. We must recognize, however, that a minority view may well continue to exist. When we unite with a minute offered by our clerk, we express, not a sudden agreement of everyone present with the prevailing view, but rather a confidence in our tried and tested way of seeking to recognise God's will. We act as a community, whose members love and trust each other. We should be reluctant to prevent the acceptance of a minute which the general body of Friends present feels to be right...

In a meeting rightly held a new way may be discovered which none present had alone perceived and which transcends the differences of the opinions expressed. This is an experience of creative insight, leading to a sense of the meeting which a clerk is often led in a remarkable way to record. Those who have shared this experience will not doubt its reality and the certainty it brings of the immediate rightness of the way for the meeting to take.

3.07

The meeting places upon its clerk a responsibility for spiritual discernment so that he or she may watch the growth of the meeting toward unity and judge the right time to submit the minute, which in its first form may serve to clear the mind of the meeting about the issues which really need its decision. In a gathering held 'in the life' there can come to the clerk a clear and unmistakable certainty about the moment to submit the minute. This may be a high peak of experience in a meeting for church affairs, but for the most part we have to wrestle with far more humdrum down-to-earth business. It must always be remembered that the final decision about whether the minute represents the sense of the meeting is the responsibility of the meeting itself, not of the clerk.

Appendix 3

Advices and Queries

Quaker Faith and Practice 1.01-1.02

As Friends we commit ourselves to a way of worship which allows God to teach and transform us. We have found corporately that the Spirit, if rightly followed, will lead us into truth, unity and love: all our testimonies grow from this leading...

Our diversity invites us both to speak what we know to be true in our lives and to learn from others. Friends are encouraged to listen to each other in humility and understanding, trusting in the Spirit that goes beyond our human effort and comprehension. So it is for the comfort and discomfort of Friends that these advices and queries are offered, with the hope that we may all be more faithful and find deeper joy in God's service:

> Dearly beloved Friends, these things we do not lay upon you as a rule or form to walk by, but that all, with the measure of light which is pure and holy, may be guided, and so in the light walking and abiding, these may be fulfilled in the Spirit, not from the letter, for the letter killeth, but the Spirit giveth life.

Postscript to an epistle to 'the brethren in the north' issued by a meeting of elders at Balby, 1656.

Advices and queries

1.02.

1. Take heed, dear Friends, to the promptings of love and truth in your hearts. Trust them as the leadings of God whose Light shows us our darkness and brings us to new life.

2. Bring the whole of your life under the ordering of the spirit

of Christ. Are you open to the healing power of God's love? Cherish that of God within you, so that this love may grow in you and guide you. Let your worship and your daily life enrich each other. Treasure your experience of God, however it comes to you. Remember that Christianity is not a notion but a way.

3. Do you try to set aside times of quiet for openness to the Holy Spirit? All of us need to find a way into silence which allows us to deepen our awareness of the divine and to find the inward source of our strength. Seek to know an inward stillness, even amid the activities of daily life. Do you encourage in yourself and in others a habit of dependence on God's guidance for each day? Hold yourself and others in the Light, knowing that all are cherished by God.

4. The Religious Society of Friends is rooted in Christianity and has always found inspiration in the life and teachings of Jesus. How to you interpret your faith in the light of this heritage? How does Jesus speak to you today? Are you following Jesus' example of love in action? Are you learning from his life the reality and cost of obedience to God? How does his relationship with God challenge and inspire you?

5. Take time to learn about other people's experiences of the Light. Remember the importance of the Bible, the writings of Friends and all writings which reveal the ways of God. As you learn from others, can you in turn give freely from what you have gained? While respecting the experiences and opinions of others, do not be afraid to say what you have found and what you value. Appreciate that doubt and questioning can also lead to spiritual growth and to a greater awareness of the Light that is in us all.

6. Do you work gladly with other religious groups in the pursuit of common goals? While remaining faithful to Quaker insights, try to enter imaginatively into the life and witness of other communities of faith, creating together the bonds of friendship.

7. Be aware of the spirit of God at work in the ordinary activities and experiences of your daily life. Spiritual learning continues throughout life, and often in unexpected ways. There is inspiration to be found all around us, in the natural world, in the sciences and arts, in our work and friendships, in our sorrows as well as in our joys. Are you open to new light, from whatever source it may come? Do you approach new ideas with discernment?

The Peace Declaration to King Charles

George Fox and other Friends, 1660[118]

Our principle is, and our practices have always been, to seek peace and ensue it and to follow after righteousness and the knowledge of God, seeking the good and welfare and doing that which tends to peace of all. We know that wars and fightings proceed from the lusts of men (as Jas iv.1-3), out of which lusts the Lord hath redeemed us, and so out of the occasion of war. The occasion of which war, and war itself (wherein envious men who are lovers of themselves more than lovers of God, lust, kill and desire to have men's lives or estates) ariseth from the lust. All bloody principles and practices, we, as to our own particulars, do utterly deny, with all outward wars and strife and fightings with outward weapons, for any end or under any pretence whatsoever. And this is our testimony to the whole world... We whom the Lord hath called into the obedience of his truth have denied wars and fightings and cannot any more learn it. This is a certain testimony unto all the world of the truth of hearts in this particular, that as God persuadeth every man's heart to believe, so they may receive it.

A translation into modern English:

Our principle is what we have always in fact practised: to seek for peace and to follow what is right and conducive to knowing God, seeking the good and welfare of all and doing what makes for peace between them. We know that fighting and war proceed from human passions – James 4:1-3 – passions from which the Lord has delivered us. So he has delivered us from the cause of war itself. The cause of war, and war itself – in which envious people, who love themselves more than God, lust after people's lives or property and (therefore) kill for it - arise from this passion. So we utterly reject all principles and practices of violence - in our own lives, that is - along with all physical war and strife, all fighting with material weapons, for any purpose or under any pretence whatever. And this is our solemn declaration to the whole world... We have rejected fighting and war because the Lord has called us to obey his truth, so we cannot now take them up again. This is a confident declaration to the whole world of the truth of our hearts in this case, in the hope that they receive it as God persuades everyone's heart to accept it.

Appendix 5

The Friends' Testimony

William Penn, 1694[119]

As their testimony was to the principle of God in man, the precious pearl and leaven of the kingdom, as the only blessed means appointed of God to quicken, convince and sanctify man, so they opened to them what it was in itself, and what it was given to them for: how they might know it from their own spirit, and that of the subtle appearance of the evil one, and what it would do for all those whose minds should be turned off from the vanity of the world, and its lifeless ways and teachers, and adhere to his blessed light in themselves, which discovers and condemns sin in all its appearances and shows how to overcome it, if minded and obeyed in its holy manifestations and convictions, giving power to such to avoid and resist those things that do not please God, and to grow strong in love, faith and good works. These things to be sure gave them a rough and disagreeable appearance with the generality, who thought them turners of the world upside down, as indeed in some sense they were, but in no other than that wherein Paul was so charged, viz. to bring things back into their primitive and right order again. For these and such like practices of theirs were not the result of humour, or for civil distinction, as some have fancied, but a fruit of inward sense, which God, through his holy fear, had begotten in them. They did not consider how to contradict the world, or distinguish themselves as a party from others, it being none of their business, as it was not their interest. No, it was not the result of consultation, or a framed design, by which to declare or recommend schism or novelty. But God having given them a sight of themselves, they saw the whole world in the same glass of truth, and sensibly discerned the affections and passions of men, and the rise and tendency of things: what it was that gratified the lust of the flesh, the lust of the eye and the pride of life, which are not of the Father but of the world. And from these sprang in the night of darkness and apostasy, which hath been over people through their degeneration from the light and spirit of God, these and many other vain customs, which are seen by the heavenly day of Christ that dawns in the soul to be either wrong in their original or, by time and abuse, hurtful in their practice. And though these things seemed trivial to some and rendered these people stingy and conceited in such persons' opinion, there was and is more in them than they were or are aware of.

Notes

1. One of the best accounts of our distinctive Way in modern times is Howard Brinton's *Guide to Quaker Practice*, Pendle Hill Publications, Wallingford, Pennsylvania, 1943.

2. My first book on Quakerism was *The End of Words: issues in contemporary Quaker theology*, Quaker Books, London, 1994, 2nd ed. 2007.

3. This small book was *Light to Live by: an exploration in Quaker spirituality*, Quaker Books, London, 2002.

4. For an accessible account of these new understandings, see John Lampen ed., *Seeing, Hearing, Knowing: reflections on Experiment with Light*, Sessions, York, 2008.

5. This only applies to Europe and to those Quakers around the world that have adopted this 'silence-based' practice. It does not really apply to those 'Evangelical Friends' who broke from that tradition in the nineteenth century.

6. The first Advice appears in the book as paragraph 1.02. The advices are also published separately in a small booklet, *Advices and Queries*, Quaker Books, London, continuously.

7. *The Book of Common Prayer* (1662), Cambridge University Press, 1968. p.v.

8. The philosopher Søren Kierkegaard, though not a Quaker himself, gave expression to just this aspiration in his *Journals*, in an entry for 1 August 1835: 'The thing is to understand myself, to see what God really wishes *me* to do; the thing is to find a truth which is true *for me*, to find *the idea for which I can live and die.*' (*The Journals of Kierkegaard 1834-1854*, selected, edited and translated by Alexander Dru, Fontana, Collins, 1958, p.44.)

9. Isaac Penington, *Flesh and Blood of Christ in the Mystery, and in the Outward* (1675), in *Works of Isaac Penington*, 3:358; also in *Knowing the Mystery of Life Within: Selected Writings of Isaac Penington in their Historical and Theological Context*, eds

R. Melvin Keiser and Rosemary Moore, Quaker Books, 2005, p. 192.

10. Thomas Hobbes, *Leviathan*, 1651, part 1, chap 13. On the significance of this book for the times see Basil Willey, *The Seventeenth Century Background*, Penguin, 1958, pp.88-110; Christopher Hill, *Puritanism and Revolution*, Secker and Warburg, 1958, pp.248-268.

11. Thomas Hobbes, as above.

12. George Fox, *The Journal*, ed. J. Nickalls, Cambridge University Press, 1952, p.11; in *TOTH* 1:13.

13. This is confirmed by an epistle that Fox wrote a few years after, in 1652: 'When your minds run into anything outwardly, without the power, it covers and veils the pure in you', Epistle 16, *Works* 7:25; in *TOTH* 1:54. I have translated this into modern English as follows: 'When your minds get taken up with something external, without reference to the power [within you], it covers and veils what is pure in you', as above

14. *TOTH* 1:75

15. George Fox, 'An Epistle to all People on the Earth', in *Doctrinals, Works* 4:132, checked by Hugh Ross against the copy of 1671 and with the word order rearranged for clarity; see Hugh MacGregor Ross, *George Fox Speaks for Himself,* Sessions, York, 1991, p.21; in *TOTH* 1:63.

16. George Fox, *Works* 4:125; *TOTH* 1:65.

17. George Fox, A Letter to Lady Claypool, 1658, in *Journal of George* Fox, ed. J.Nickalls, Cambridge University Press, 1952, p. 346; in *TOTH* 1:61.

18. George Fox, A paper of 1656, in *Journal*, ed. Ellwood, in *Works* 1:295; *TOTH* 1:82.

19. On this special sense of 'objectivity' see the Quaker psychologist, Adam Curle, *Mystics and Militants: a Study of Awareness, Identity and Social Action*, Tavistock Publications, 1972, pp. 18, 107.

20. George Fox, Epistle 358 (1679), *Works* 8:165; in *TOTH* 3:84. The text reads (in part), 'Truth... makes all like itself that do obey it, universal, to live out of narrowness and self, and deny it. So it brings all into oneness and answers the good principle of God in all people'.

21. Adam Curle, *True Justice*, Quaker Home Service, 1981, p. 92.

22. George Fox, Epistle 55 (1653), *Works* 7:71; in *TOTH* 1:122

23. Even Martin Luther was able to accept, in his Catechism, that the meaning of God is related to our human need: 'God is whatever your heart cleaves to'; Paul Tillich was following Luther when he defined God as 'our ultimate concern'.

24. See David Boulton, ed., *Godless for God's Sake: nontheism in contemporary Quakerism*, Dent Cumbria, 2006.

25. *TOTH*, 1:7.

26. Also in the anthology, as above.

27. *TOTH* 1:4.

28. Samuel Fisher, *Apokrypta Apokalypta*, 1660, in *Early Quaker Writings (EQW)*, eds Barbour and Roberts, pp.306f.

29. Margaret Fell (later to be married to George Fox), 'The testimony of Margaret Fox concerning her late husband', in George Fox, *The Journal*, 1694, p.ii; bicent edn, 1891, vol 2, pp 512-514; not in Nickalls edn; also in *Quaker Faith and Practice*, (2008) 19.07.

30. George Fox, 'A word from the Lord to all the world' (1654?), in *Doctrinals, Works* 4:38f; in *TOTH* 1:92. There are echoes here of some mystical writing in the Middle Ages. Consider e.g. a passage from the English text of the fourteenth century (author unknown) *The Cloud of Unknowing*, chapter 14: 'Swink and sweat in all that thou canst and mayest, for to get thee a true knowing and a feeling of thyself as thou art; and then I trow that soon after that thou shalt have a true knowing and a feeling of God as He is'. I could translate this into modern English as follows: 'Try as hard

as you can to get a real knowledge and sense of yourself as you are, and then, I promise you, you will soon get a true knowledge and sense of God as he is'.

31. Samuel Fisher, *Apokakrypta Apokalypta*, 1660, in *EQW*, p. 307f.

32. Quoted in Roberts Vaux, *Memoirs of the Life of Anthony Benezet*, Philadelphia, 1817, pp.107f.

33. William Penn, 'Some Fruits of Solitude' (1693), reprinted in *William Penn*, ed. Edwin B. Bronner, *The Peace of Europe, The Fruits of Solitude and Other Writings*, Everyman, 1993, p.60.

34. Penn seems to be alluding to Paul the Apostle here, specifically 1 Corinthians 13; 12 (in the Authorized, King James version): 'Now we see through a glass, darkly; but then face to face: now I know in part; but then shall I know even as also I am known'; and 2 Corinthians 3:18: 'We all, with open face beholding as in a glass the glory of the Lord, are changed into the same image from glory to glory even as by the Spirit of the Lord'.

35. Job 1:21 (REB).

36. Isaac Penington, *The Works*, 3:458, (1670?), reprinted by Quaker Heritage Press, Pennsylvania, 1996.

37. George Fox, Epistle 215 (1661), *Works* 7:215; also in *TOTH*, 2:82.

38. This modern experience, which gives shape to our spiritual needs, is well described by Heije Faber, *Above the Treeline: towards a contemporary spirituality*, SCM Press, 1988.

39. *QFP* 6.02. This first (regular) meeting of Friends from across the whole country took place in 1668. The meetings that took place 'formerly', from 1654 to 1667, were occasional, being threatened always by persecution.

40. This experience is explored philosophically be Emmanuel Levinas, *Totality and Infinity*, Kluwer Academic Publishers, 1991, pp.187-253. Although not a Quaker himself, Levinas begins to sound like one in this book, and his subtle philos-

ophizing helps to articulate this aspect of the Quaker experience. He outlines his view more accessibly in *Ethics and Infinity*, Duquesne University Press, Pittsburgh, 1985, pp.83-90, and it is discussed briefly by Heije Faber, *Above the Treeline: towards a contemporary spirituality*, SCM Press, 1988, pp.64-81.

41. George Fox, Epistle 244 (1666), in *Works* 2:274; also in *TOTH* 2:74

42. George Fox, Epistle 18 (1652), in *Works* 7:25f; also in *TOTH* 3:27.

43. *QFP* 10.03. Emphasis mine.

44. Patricia Loring, *Listening Spirituality: volume 1, Personal Spiritual Practices among Friends* (1997); *volume 2, Corporal Spiritual Practice among Friends* (1999), Openings Press, Washington DC.

45. *QFP* 2.35. The reference to Fox is Epistle 149, 'To Friends, to know one another in the Light', 1657, in *Works* 7:141.

46. Samuel Fisher, *Apokakrypta* in *Early Quaker Writings*, pp.306f.

47. George Fox, Epistle 320, 'An encouragement to all the faithful women's meetings in the world, who assemble together in the fear of God for the service of truth', 1676, *Works* 8.96; in *TOTH* 2:30.

48. See Hugh Barbour and J. William Frost, *The Quakers*, pp. 203-218.

49. George Fox, Epistle 320 (1676), *Works* 8:97; *TOTH* 2:32. Cf. 1 Peter 4:10.

50. Isaac Penington, Letter 21, 1667; in *QFP* 10:27.

51. *QFP* 10.05.

52. George Fox, a paper of 1654, in *Doctrinals, Works* 4:43; in *TOTH* 2:18.

53. The above quotation from the 1654 paper continues: 'And who know the light are in unity; all who know the word, which is mystery, are come to the beginning, are sanctified

by the word, and clear through the word; for the word is a fire... The light and the word... working out that filthy nature which the outward law takes hold on; so walking in the spirit, there is no fulfilling of the lusts...' So the light is also now a 'fire' and 'the spirit'. These are evidently different descriptions of the same inner, divine source according to how it affects human experience. The light shows, the word speaks, the fire burns up, and so on, describing inner experiences of enlightenment, under-standing and purification respectively.

54. George Fox, as above; in *TOTH* 2.18.

55. See my notes on 'gospel' and 'gospel order' in the Glossary of *Truth of the Heart* pp.158f, and the discussion in the Essay, pp.190-192.

56. The problem of conflict in Quaker meetings seems to be growing as the old disciplines of listening and truth-telling are being forgotten, or no longer taught. See research on this from Susan Robson, 'Grasping the Nettle: Conflict and the Quaker Condition', in eds Pink Dandelion and Peter Collins, *The Quaker Condition: the Sociology of a Liberal Religion*, Cambridge Scholars Publishing, Newcastle, 2008, pp.140-157

57. George Fox, Epistle 340 (1676), *Works* 8:131; in *TOTH* 2:96

58. *QFP* 2.41

59. George Fox, Epistle 249 (1667), *Works* 7:292; in *TOTH* 1:33.

60. George Fox, Epistle 260 (1668), *Works* 7:317; in *TOTH* 1:34.

61. Robert Barclay, *Apology*, 1676, Proposition 11, para 7.

62. George Fox, An Epistle to Friends of 1658, in his *Journal*, ed. Nickalls, pp.340ff; also in *Works* 1:366f; in *TOTH* 2:15

63. *QFP* 1.02, Advice 8. Cf. *QFP* 2.01: 'Worship is the response of the human spirit to the presence of the divine and eternal, to the God who first seeks us. The sense of wonder and awe of the finite before the infinite leads naturally to thanksgiving and adoration'.

64. A large tavern near St. Paul's Cathedral
65. The women's meetings were not appointed until ten years later.
66. Edward Burrough, *A Testimony Concerning the Beginning of the Work of the Lord... in this City of London,* a paper of 1662; reprinted in 1841 by Abram Barclay in his ed., *Letters Etc. of Early Friends,* pp. 299f, 305, but not since, apart from an extract in our current *Quaker Faith and Practice,* 2.87. The passage quoted, or part of it, is discussed by Michael Sheeran, in his *Beyond Majority Rule,* p. 4
67. Barry Morley, *Beyond Consensus,* Pendle Hill Publications, Philadephia, 1993, p.5. It seems to be an American style to speak of 'sense of the meeting' without the 'a' or 'the' before it.
68. *TOTH,* 1:68
69. In *TOTH,* 1:81
70. Barry Morley, *Beyond Consensus,* p. 16.
71. Michael Sheeran, *Beyond Majority Rule,* pp. 57f
72. Michael Sheeran, *Beyond Majority Rule,* p. 58
73. Barry Morley, *Beyond Consensus,* p. 13
74. *QFP,* 3.06.
75. Barry Morley, *Beyond Consensus,* pp. 19f
76. George Fox, *Journal,* ed. John Nickalls, p. 346
77. George Fox, Epistle 200 ('On justice', 1661), *Works* 7:193; in *TOTH,* 3:48
78. M.K.Gandhi, *From Yeravda Mandir: ashram observances,* Navvajivan, Ahmedabad, 1957, p.8. The Sanskrit term Gandhi uses for 'love' is *ahimsa,* which would normally be translated 'nonviolence'. But the context makes it clear that Gandhi had the broader meaning in mind. At this point he was very close to Quakers in his spirituality, as he himself recognized.
79. Published in America in 1943, and many times since
80. Thomas Kelly, 'The simplification of life', in *A Testament of*

Devotion, Hodder and Stoughton, 1943, p.96

81. As above, pp.96f.
82. As above, p. 98
83. Donald Court, in *QFP* 20.09 from the year 1970.
84. Rex Ambler, *Light to Live by*, Quaker Books, second edition, 2007
85. A testimony to the life of Mary Hughes, in *QFP* 18.13.
86. On clearness committees see Patricia Loring, *Spiritual Discernment*, Pendle Hill Pamphlets, 1992; and her *Listening Spirituality; vol 2, Corporate Spiritual Practices among Friends;* also *QFP* 12.20.
87. Elizabeth Bathurst, *An Epistle to such Friends of Christ as have lately been Convinced of the Truth*, 1679, reprinted in her collected works, *Truth Vindicated*, 1695, and again in ed. Mary Garman et al. *Hidden in Plain Sight: Quaker Women's Writings 1650-1700*, Pendle Hill, Wallingford PA. 1996, p. 429
88. See Pink Dandelion, *An Introduction to Quakerism*, Cambridge University Press, 2007, pp.129-152
89. 1 John 1:1-3.
90. *TOTH* 1:63
91. Ephesians 4:15
92. This has been shown in Owen Watkins' excellent book, *The Puritan Experience*, 1970. Augustine's *Confessions* was perhaps the first of this genre, and that was written over a thousand years before, but it was a remarkable one-off; it didn't set a trend like the journals of the first Quakers.
93. *Primitive Christianity Revived*, 1696, reprinted in William Penn, *The Peace of Europe, the Fruits of Solitude and other Writings*, ed. Edwin Bronner, Everyman, 1993, pp.227f.
94. *TOTH* 3:32
95. George Fox, *Journal* (for 1661), ed. John Nickalls, pp.409f
96. This translation, with the original text, is from my anthology, *TOTH* 3:71.
97. George Fox, A letter 'to Friends in the ministry', 1656, in

Journal, ed. John Nickalls, p.263; also in *TOTH* 3:37.

98. This text, though written with other Friends, was included in Fox's *Journal*, ed. John Nickalls, pp.399f; also in *TOTH* 3:42. See Appendix 4 for a translation into modern English, which also appeared in *TOTH*.

99. George Fox, Epistle 315 (1675), *Works of George Fox*, vol.8, p.75; in *Truth of the Heart*, 3:38.

100. On the traditional testimonies see the current *Quaker Faith and Practice* (4ᵗʰ edition 2009), chapters 20 and 24; on community chapters 16, 17 and 22; and on the newly emerging concern for the earth, chapter 25.

101. James Nayler, *Works* p.46.

102. See end of chapter on 'Living Faithfully'.

103. John Woolman, *The Journal and Essays of John Woolman*, ed. Phillips P. Moulton, 1971, pp. 127f. (journal entry for '12ᵗʰ day, 6th month' 1763); also in *QFP* 27:02.

104. I Corinthians 13:9.

105. *TOTH* 3:9.

106. William Penn, *The Rise and Progress of the People called Quakers*, first published as a preface to Fox's *Journal* (1694), but later published separately; recently republished in William Penn (ed. Edwin Bonner), *The Peace of Europe, the Fruits of Solitude and other Writings*, Everyman, 1993, p.286.

107. I have written more fully on this elsewhere, in 'Darkness and light', in *God and Evil: Quaker perspectives*, eds. Jackie Leach Scully and Pink Dandelion, Ashgate, 2007, pp.193-206.

108. Nikos Kazantzakis, *Report to Greco*, translated by Peter Bien, (a Quaker, as it happens), Faber and Faber, p.343.

109. William Penn, *The Peace of Europe, the Fruits of Solitude and other Writings*, Everyman, 1993, p.278.

110. Václav Havel, *Living the Truth*, Faber and Faber, 1983, pp.57f. (emphasis mine).

111. See the end of the previous chapter, 'Bearing witness'.

112. Swarthmoor MS, iii, 145, Friends House Library; quoted in Barry Reay, *The Quakers and the English Revolution*, Temple Smith, London, 1985, p.100.

113. See Clarence Yarrow, *Quaker Experience in International Conciliation*, New Haven, USA, 1978.

114. See Adam Curle's account of his own experience in *Making Peace*, Tavistock Publications, 1971.

115. See James Walvin's book on the subject, *A Short History of Slavery*, Penguin, 2007, especially chapter 10.

116. Samuel Fisher, *Apokrypta Apokalypta*, 1660, in *Early Quaker Writings*, ed. Barbour and Roberts, pp.306f.

117. *QPF* 3.02 – 3.07.

118. George Fox, *The Journal*, ed. John Nickalls, pp.399f; also in *TOTH* 3:42.

119. *The Rise and Progress of the People called Quakers*, first published as a preface to Fox's Journal, but later published separately; recently republished in ed. Edwin Bronner, *The Peace of Europe, the Fruits of Solitude and other Writings*, Everyman, 1993, pp.278, 286f.

References

Ambler, Rex, *Truth of the Heart: an anthology of George Fox*, with a translation into modern English and an interpretive essay, Quaker Books, London, 2nd edition, 2007.

Ambler, Rex, *Light to Live by: an exploration of Quaker spirituality*, Quaker Books, London, 2nd edition, 2008.

Ambler, Rex, *The End of Words: issues in contemporary Quaker theology*, Quaker Books, London, 2nd edition, 2004.

Barbour, Hugh, and J. William Frost, *The Quakers*, Friends United Press, Richmond, Indiana, 1994 (first published by Greenwood Press, Conn., 1988).

Barbour, Hugh, and Arthur O. Roberts, *Early Quaker Writings*, Pendle Hill Publications, 2nd printing, 2007.

Barclay, Abram, ed., *Letters Etc. of Early Friends*, Harvey and Darton, London, 1841.

Barclay, Robert, *An Apology for the True Christian Divinity*, London, Latin edition 1676, English edition 1678.

Bathurst, Elizabeth, *Truth Vindicated*, London, 1695.

Boulton, David, ed. *Godless for God's Sake: nontheism in contemporary Quakerism*, Dent, Cumbria, England, 2006.

Braithwaite, William C., *The Beginnings of Quakerism*, Macmillan, 1912; 2nd edition, Cambridge University Press, 1955; reprinted Sessions, York, England, 1981.

Brinton, Howard, *A Guide to Quaker Practice*, Pendle Hill Publications, Wallingford, Pennsylvania, 1943.

Britain Yearly Meeting of the Religious Society of Friends, *Quaker Faith and Practice*, 4th edition, 1995-2008.

Britain Yearly Meeting, *Advices and Queries*, 4th edition, 1995-2008.

Burrough, Edward, *A Testimony Concerning the Beginning of the Work of the Lord... in this City of London*, London, 1662.

Church of England, *The Book of Common Prayer* (1662), Cambridge

University Press, 1968.

Curle, Adam, *Making Peace,* Tavistock Publications, London, 1971.

Curle, Adam, *Mystics and Militants: a study of awareness, identity and social action,* Tavistock Publications, London,1972.

Curle, Adam, *True Justice,* Quaker Home Service, London,1981.

Dandelion, Pink, *An Introduction to Quakerism,* Cambridge University Press, 2007.

Dandelion, Pink and Peter Collins, eds, *The Quaker Condition: the sociology of a liberal religion,* Cambridge Scholars Publishing, Newcastle, England, 2008.

Faber, Heije, *Above the Treeline: towards a contemporary spirituality,* SCM Press, London, 1988.

Fox, George, *The Works of George Fox,* 8 volumes, Gould, Philadelphia, 1831, reprinted by New Foundation Publication, Pennsylvania, 1990.

Fox, George, *The Journal,* ed. John Nickalls, Cambridge University Press, 1952.

Gandhi, M.K., *From Yeravda Mandir: ashram observances,* Navajivan Press, Ahmedabad, 1957.

Garman, Mary, et. al., *Hidden in Plain Sight: Quaker women's writings 1650-1700,* Pendle Hill Publications, Wallingford, Pennsylvania, 1996.

Havel, Václav, *Living the Truth,* Faber and Faber, 1983.

Hill, Christopher, *Puritanism and Revolution,* Secker and Warburg, 1958.

Hobbes, Thomas, *Leviathan,* 1651.

Kazantzakis, Nikos, *Report to Greco,* translated by Peter Bien, Bruno Cassirer, Oxford, England, 1972.

Keiser, R. Melvin, and Rosemary Moore, eds, *Knowing the Mystery of Life Within: selected writings of Isaac Penington in their historical and theological context,* Quaker Books, London, 2005.

Kelly, Thomas, *A Testament of Devotion,* Hodder and Stoughton, 1943.

Kierkegaard, Søren, *Journals 1834-1854,* edited and translated by

Alexander Dru, Fontana Books, Collins, 1958.

Lampen, John, ed., *Seeing, Hearing, Knowing: reflections of Experiment with Light,* Sessions, York, 2008.

Leach Scully, Jackie, and Pink Dandelion, eds., *Good and Evil: Quaker perspectives,* Ashgate, 2007.

Levinas, Emmanuel, *Totality and Infinity,* Kluwer Academic Publishers, 1991.

Levinas, Emmanuel, *Ethics and Infinity,* Duquesne University Press, Pittsburgh, 1985.

Loring, Patricia, *Spiritual Discernment: the context and goal of clearness committees,* Pendle Hill Publications, Wallingford, Pennsylvania, 1992.

Loring, Patricia, *Listening Spirituality: volume 1, Personal Spiritual Practices among Friends* (1997); *volume 2, Corporal Spiritual Practice among Friends* (1999), Openings Press, Washington DC.

Morley, Barry, *Beyond Consensus: salvaging sense of the meeting,* Pendle Hill Publications, Wallingford, Pennsylvania, 1993.

Nayler, James, *The Works,* London, 1716.

Penington, Isaac, *The Works,* 4 vols, 4th edition 1863, reprinted by Quaker Heritage Press, Glenside, Pennsylvania, 1996.

Penn, William, *The Peace of Europe, The Fruits of Solitude and Other Writings,* ed. Edwin B. Bronner, Everyman, Dent, 1993.

Quaker Life Study Pack, *Quaker Identity and the Heart of our Faith,* Quaker Books, 2nd edition 2009.

Reay, Barry, *The Quakers and the English Revolution,* Temple Smith, London, 1985.

Ross, Hugh MacGregor, *George Fox Speaks for Himself,* Sessions, York, England, 1991.

Sheeran, Michael, *Beyond Majority Rule: voteless decisions in the Religious Society of Friends,* Philadelphia Yearly Meeting of the Religious Society of Friends, 1983.

Vaux, Roberts, *Memoirs of the Life of Anthony Benezet,* Philadelphia, 1817.

Walvin, James, *A Short History of Slavery*, Penguin, 2007.

Watkins, Owen, *The Puritan Experience: studies in spiritual autobiography*, Routledge and Kegan Paul, London, 1972.

Willey, Basil, *The Seventeenth Century Background*, Penguin, 1958.

Woolman, John, *The Journal and Essays of John Woolman*, ed. Phillips Moulton, Oxford University Press, 1971.

Yarrow, Clarence, *Quaker Experience in International Conciliation*, New Haven, Conn., 1978.

Further reading

Barbour, Hugh, *The Quakers in Puritan England,* Yale University Press, 1964.

Barbour, Hugh, and J. William Frost, *The Quakers,* Friends United Press, Richmond, Indiana, 1994 (first published by Greenwood Press, Conn., 1988).

Britain Yearly Meeting of the Religious Society of Friends, *Quaker Faith and Practice,* 4th edition, 1995-2008.

Durham, Geoffrey, *The Spirit of the Quakers: an anthology,* Yale University Press, 2010.

Hamm, Thomas D., *Quaker Writings: an anthology, 1650-1920,* Penguin Classics, 2010.

CHRISTIAN
ALTERNATIVE

Throughout the two thousand years of Christian tradition there
have been, and still are, groups and individuals that exist in the
margins and upon the edge of faith. But in Christianity's
contrapuntal history it has often been these outcasts and
pioneers that have forged contemporary orthodoxy out of
former radicalism as belief evolves to engage with and
encompass the ever-changing social and scientific realities. Real
faith lies not in the comfortable certainties of the Orthodox, but
somewhere in a half-glimpsed hinterland on the dirt track to
Emmaus, where the Death of God meets the Resurrection, where
the supernatural Christ meets the historical Jesus, and where the
revolution liberates both the oppressed and the oppressors.

Welcome to Christian Alternative... a space at the edge where
the light shines through.